LÉA ROBACK

Abstract

Léa Roback (1903–2000), who was my great-aunt, was well known for her seven decades of activist work in Quebec, especially her union and women's rights activism. This biography provides readers with an opportunity to read about Roback's activist life and work from the perspective of one of her great-nieces, who is an activist herself. At a time when the geopolitical moment has produced polarized views and a lack of dialogue, Roback's ability to cross linguistic, religious, cultural, and class borders – in order to work towards social justice needs to be documented and shared. The biography will be of interest to educators and social justice activists around the world.

Key words

Access to abortion – Quebec, Canada; Activism – Quebec, Canada; Anti-apartheid – South Africa; Communist Party – Canada; Jewish history – Canada; Peace activism – Quebec, Canada; Quebec history – Canada; Union labour history – Quebec, Canada; Women's history – Quebec, Canada; Women's right to vote – Quebec, Canada

Contents

Acknowledgements		viii
Warning		ix
Learning objectives		x
Chapter 1	Léa Roback: Her life and times (1903–2000)	1
Chapter 2	Beauport and Montreal: Family and community life (1905–1929)	23
Chapter 3	Berlin and Montreal: Political learning and Communist Party work (1929–1958)	53
Chapter 4	Montreal: Fighting for workers' rights (1936–1952)	75
Chapter 5	Montreal: Fighting for women's rights (1933–2000)	99
Chapter 6	Léa Roback: Growing older (1988–2000)	131
Notes		151
Discussion questions		157
References		159
Recommended further reading		167
Index		172

Acknowledgements

There are many people who supported the research and writing of this biography, and I'd like to thank and acknowledge them.

First, I'd like to acknowledge the people who read early and later drafts of the biography and provided excellent feedback, which helped shape the final manuscript: Sophie Bissonnette, Margot Huycke, Melanie Leavitt, and Judith Roback.

The archival research staff at the Jewish Public Library in Montreal – Eddie Paul, Maya Pasternak, and Sam Pappas – provided me with expert guidance on how to navigate the wide variety of material about Auntie Léa's life and activism housed there. After collecting and scanning the material I wanted to use in the biography, my research team – Noah Lee, Jesse Scott, Mia Jakobsen, and Anya Shen – supported the organization, translation and transcription of some of the material.

I also want to acknowledge and thank publisher David Parker and series editor Anna Hayward at Lived Places Publishing for their support in completing the final draft of the biography. As the book went into production, the Lived Places Publishing team worked with me to ensure that the book was polished and error-free.

Finally, of course, I want to acknowledge and thank my great-aunt Léa for spending her entire life fighting for workers' and women's rights and leaving behind a better world for us to inherit. It's our turn now to continue the fight and leave behind a better world for the generations to come.

Warning

This biography contains explicit references to, and descriptions of, situations which may cause distress. This includes references to and descriptions of:

- Genocide
- Sexual assault
- Ableism, discrimination, and microaggressions

Learning objectives

1. To read about the life and activist work of Léa Roback (1903–2000), who was involved in some of the most important social issues of the twentieth century, and to understand history from the storytelling of an elder from Quebec.
2. To recognize and discuss how Léa Roback's life experiences as a child, adolescent, and young adult influenced her life work as an activist.
3. To describe and discuss how Léa Roback's ability to cross borders facilitated her advocacy and activism against anti-semitism, classism, sexism, racism, and heterosexism and made it forceful.
4. To name the ways Léa Roback's advocacy was characterized by activist community care.
5. To discuss what educators and activists today can learn from Léa Roback's advocacy and activism, and how they can integrate Roback's approaches and strategies in their social justice work.

1
Léa Roback
Her life and times (1903–2000)

"Knitting isn't my passion – social causes are."

– Léa Roback[1]

***

My great-aunt Léa Roback was a force. She was brave, bold, fiercely intelligent, well-read, politically astute, and funny. Like her sister, my grandmother Rose, and the other Roback siblings, Auntie Léa was a compelling storyteller, and much of what I knew about the injustices in the world in my childhood and adolescence came from listening to my family, and Auntie Léa herself, tell stories about her activist work. Social causes were Auntie Léa's passion.[2]

My cousin Melanie Leavitt, a public historian who leads walking tours in Montreal about the Jewish left movement in the 1930s and 1940s describes Auntie Léa as a trailblazing feminist, labour organizer, communist, and peace activist whose activism spanned seven decades. In the 2024 podcast *recollections* produced by the Jewish Public Library about the history of the Jewish Left in Montreal, Leavitt says Auntie Léa pretty much saw every important moment in the Left throughout the twentieth century. She was a fixture in marches and at protests well into the 1980s and 1990s and she never retired from her commitment to social justice work.

> It was a lifelong commitment and it's interesting because Léa was somebody who was never one who would rest on her laurels of past accomplishments. She was always adapting and evolving with changing times and with changing concerns and always very open to looking at who are the present-day people who are being marginalized? "Where is my attention and my activism most needed now?" (Jewish Public Library, 2024c, *recollections*, Episode 3).

For Leavitt, Auntie Léa's openness to new ideas was one of her great strengths as an activist. It prevented her activism from becoming fossilized. Another great strength was Auntie Léa's ability to build bridges between communities. She spoke Yiddish, French, and English fluently, which enabled her to connect with multiple communities – Anglophone, Francophone, Jewish, Catholic, Protestant, middle-class, and working-class – first in the labour and suffrage movements of the 1930s and 1940s and then in the anti-war and women's movements between the 1960s and 1990s.

Born to a Jewish immigrant family on 3 November 1903, in Montreal, Auntie Léa grew up in the rural French-speaking community of Beauport, just outside Quebec City, where her parents ran a small general store. Like other Jewish families from Eastern Europe living in French-speaking communities, Auntie Léa learned to speak Yiddish at home, French to the neighbours, and English at school. She remained fluent in all three languages all her life and was able to easily switch back and forth among them.

Coming from a Jewish family, Auntie Léa and her eight brothers and sisters were not permitted to attend the local French Catholic elementary school in Beauport because they were not Catholic. In the early 1900s, the school system in Quebec was separated by religion. Children being raised in Catholic families went to Catholic elementary and secondary schools. Children raised in Protestant families went to Protestant schools.

At the time, Jews living in Quebec didn't have the same constitutional rights to education as Protestants and Catholics did. However, in 1903, the Quebec provincial government created a stipulation in the Education Act which designated Jews living in Quebec as "honorary Protestants" for educational purposes so that Protestant School Boards in the province could receive funding for Jewish students. This was because by 1901 the Jewish population in Montreal had reached 7,000 people, and there were more and more Jewish children going to Protestant schools. A decade later, the Montreal Jewish community quadrupled to 28,000 people and represented five percent of the city's population. While most Jewish immigrants in Quebec settled in Montreal, some families made homes in other cities and rural communities – Quebec City, Trois-Rivières, Sherbrooke, Joliette. Like the Roback family, most of these families made a living by running small retail businesses (Anctil and Woodsworth, 2021, pp. 62, 69).

Every day from Monday to Friday, Auntie Léa and her siblings took a train from their French-speaking Catholic community in Beauport to go to an English Protestant school in Quebec City. They started the school day by singing the British national anthem, "God Save the King," reciting the Protestant Lord's Prayer, and singing one or two Christian hymns. At the end of the school day, they took a train back home to Beauport. Travelling between a Yiddish-speaking Jewish home, a French-speaking Catholic community, and an English-speaking Protestant school as a child gave Auntie Léa linguistic and cultural skills that became foundational to her future activist work in Quebec.

Beauport was a town that was Catholic as well as French-speaking, and when they arrived, the Roback family were the first and only Jewish family in the village. As Melanie Leavitt explains, growing up Jewish in Beauport assisted Auntie Léa later on in life to build bridges between communities.

> She ends up spending her formative years from the age of around two years old until she's 15, living in this, immersed in this traditional French-Canadian rural setting. And because of that experience, she is exposed to [its] culture. She's exposed not only to the language, but also to understanding the cultural background of traditional early 20th century Quebec society. Something that very few other Jewish members of the Jewish community would be exposed to (Jewish Public Library, 2024c, *recollections,* Episode 3).

Auntie Léa's memories of growing up in Beauport, and her reflections on how her early family and community life influenced her later activism, are shared in Chapter 2.

In 1919, the Roback family moved from Beauport back to Montreal. Auntie Léa was 15, and she went to work for British American Dyeworks, a cleaning and dyeing company, as a front desk receptionist. The Robacks were a working-class family and needed Auntie Léa's income to pay the bills. At British American Dyeworks, Auntie Léa learned about the social stratification between the English Protestant elite and the French Catholic working class in Montreal. Every day she witnessed the inequalities that existed between the elite English customers who had their maids and drivers bring in their clothes for cleaning and the poorly paid French workers who did the cleaning. As Melanie Leavitt explains:

> Here you have these workers coming in [to British American Dyeworks]. It's oftentimes what would be referred to as 'la bonne', you know, the maid, the housekeeper, or the drivers coming in, and they're bringing in dresses that belong to the upper class, the elite, the bourgeoisie of Montreal society. And she's ... looking at these dresses that most likely cost what these working, like what the working class would make in a year ... [it's an] example that highlights ... not only class divisions, but how [class divisions] also fall along language lines and along religious lines as well (Jewish Public Library, 2024c, *recollections*, Episode 3).

In her book *Remembrances of Grandeur*, Margaret Westley describes the families who made up the Anglo-Protestant elite of Montreal at this time (Westley, 1991). The group was small and included people such as Sir Hugh Allan, Peter McGill, the Molsons, George Stephens, and Richard Angus, all of whom lived in mansions built on the slopes of Mount Royal, "the Mountain." Sir Hugh Allan was a shipping and railway magnate. Peter McGill founded the first railway company in Canada. The Molsons founded Canada's oldest and largest brewery. George Stephens was the

President of Canadian Pacific Railway (CPR). Richard Angus was one of the founding directors of CPR. Westley estimates that in the 1890s, between 50 and 150 Montrealers owned almost two-thirds of the wealth of the entire country.

After leaving British American Dyeworks, Auntie Léa became a cashier at His Majesty's Theatre, where she was introduced to the contemporary repertoire of English and French theatre. Already a devotee of Yiddish theatre and literature, Auntie Léa began to develop a lifelong passion for English and French theatre and literature as well. Five years later, at the age of 27, Auntie Léa left Montreal to study French literature at the Université de Grenoble in France, where she worked as an English tutor to pay for her classes. It was extremely unusual for a young woman in her twenties to sail from Montreal to Europe alone at the time, and a good story about Auntie Léa's boat trip appears in Chapter 3. Growing up listening to stories about Auntie Léa's adventures in Europe gave me a different vision of how a woman's life might be led. A young woman could get on a boat and travel to Europe to study and see the world. She didn't have to get married in her twenties, have children, and raise a family. In fact, Auntie Léa never married. She never wanted to.

> I went out. I had boyfriends. I always said, "I'm damned if I'm going to get up to make breakfast for a guy. He can make breakfast for himself – *qu'il s'arrange*. I'll take all the loving I can get, and the attention, but the housecleaning and meals – that's not in my dictionary. I liked to be friendly with the guys and if they were nice, we made love – *après tout, c'est la vie* – and life was very exciting and interesting" (Schwartz and Roback, 1996/1997, p. 6).

Although Auntie Léa started a Bachelor of Arts degree in Grenoble, she didn't finish the program. It was an excellent experience, says Melanie Leavitt, but it didn't quite live up to what she had hoped it would be. By 1929, she had moved to Berlin.

> And that's the next, I'd say, pivotal moment in her life as a left-wing activist. She joins her brother, her older brother Harry, who was studying medicine in Berlin. And once she's in Berlin, that's her exposure to … the economic Great Depression, [and] also the rise of fascism (Jewish Public Library, 2024c, *recollections,* Episode 3).[3]

In Berlin, Auntie Léa enrolled in university again, learned German, explored the city and joined the Communist Party because it was the only political party that was taking concrete action against massive unemployment, the economic crisis, and fascism. The Socialists, for example, would hold meetings and talk about what might be done but didn't act. Auntie Léa always said she hated meetings. She wanted to act, to do something. Leavitt tells us:

> … the only really legitimate response that she's seeing to this rise of fascism is from the Communist Party. And so that's where she first develops her interest in the kind of actions that they're taking on the streets. She participates in the May Day demonstrations and witnesses police brutality against the Left, but this sort of solidifies her political convictions.
>
> She said it was a baptism by fire when she decides to join the Communist Party. She ends up officially joining the Communist Party in Berlin in 1931. And so, she's immersed in the ideology [the ideas and beliefs of Communism]. There's a lot of education about the issues

[of the day] (Jewish Public Library, 2024c, *recollections*, Episode 3).

Auntie Léa gained a political education when she joined the Communist Party in Berlin. As someone who was not afraid to step out of line, break the rules, and speak out against injustices, the Party provided her with a space and structure to act and push for change. After returning to Montreal from Berlin, Auntie Léa joined the Communist Party of Canada, but being a "free spirit" as documentary filmmaker Sophie Bissonnette described her to me, she also felt profoundly accountable to and in tune with the rank and file she worked with. Auntie Léa would become critical of the Party and eventually leave when she felt it no longer served the needs of the people whose causes she embraced.

When Hitler came into power in 1933, the political climate in Berlin became increasingly hostile to Jews living in Germany. Auntie Léa was a Jewish woman, a member of the Communist Party, and a foreigner. Her friends and comrades in the Communist movement advised her to leave Germany and return to Canada.

"She's very resistant at first," says Melanie Leavitt. "She's somebody who is very tenacious. She is fearless. She always wants to be on the front lines and fighting against injustice. But she quickly realizes that she has to return to Canada" (Jewish Public Library, 2024c, *recollections*, Episode 3).

So, at the end of 1932, Auntie Léa escaped Germany "by the skin of [her] teeth" (Weisbord, 2022, p.46) and returned to Montreal, which had become a very different city from the one she'd left in the 1920s. The Jewish community she returned to was also different from the one she left. Melanie Leavitt explains:

> She's arriving back at a time when there is rampant poverty and unemployment and major suffering. But also at the same time, because of the dire circumstances, there's also a groundswell of support for various different left-wing movements … she's able to return to a Montreal and a Jewish left-wing Montreal that's already actively engaged.
>
> And that's when she joins into the activities and the organizing that's taking place here by the Communist Party here in Montreal and in Quebec. And immediately, you know, she meets somebody like Fred Rose, who at the time was the leader of the Quebec Division of the Communist Party. And so, it's right away back into the heart of the action (Jewish Public Library, 2024c, *recollections,* Episode 3).

In Chapter 3, I share what Auntie Léa learned during her years in Berlin. I also share her stories about returning to Montreal and her work for the Communist Party.

As a member of the Communist Party in Montreal, Auntie Léa opened a leftist bookstore. Her work for the Party led to an invitation to become the Educational Director of the International Ladies' Garment Workers Union (ILGWU). In this position, Auntie Léa recruited thousands of women members for the ILGWU. Then in 1937, she co-led 5,000 garment workers – most of them women – on a three-week strike for better pay and working conditions. After the strike was over, Auntie Léa worked for the ILGWU as a Grievance Officer. When she left the ILGWU in 1939, Auntie Léa went to work at the RCA factory in St. Henri and organized the workers there. These accomplishments are discussed in Chapter 4. In Chapter 5, I discuss Auntie Léa's activist work in the Quebec suffrage movement, peace movement, anti-apartheid movement, anti-pornography movement, and access to abortion movement.

Auntie Léa remained an activist well into her 80s and 90s. In the last chapter, I talk about the ways Auntie Léa lived out the last years of her life and discuss the many tributes and honours she has received for her work. I also discuss the way Auntie Léa's activism continues to live on in the generations of educators and activists who have followed her.

Perspectives in the biography
Intersectionality

As an activist who was always adapting and evolving with changing times, Auntie Léa was never a single-issue activist. She understood the importance of what today is known as "intersectionality." The idea of intersectionality emerged in the early 1980s and is often credited to Audre Lorde who was a Black feminist lesbian scholar and poet from the United States. Lorde challenged her readers to think about the ways identity, politics and activism around different social identities and issues were connected and related to each other. In her essay, "There is No Hierarchy of Oppressions" (1983) for example, Lorde argued it was not possible to gain a meaningful picture or understanding of a person's experience by only examining a single dimension of their identity, for example, their racial or sexual identity. It was also not possible to gain a meaningful understanding of the discrimination or oppression a person was facing without considering multiple dimensions of their identity. Lorde famously wrote:

> Any attack against Black people is a lesbian and gay issue, because I and thousands of other Black women are part of the lesbian community. Any attack against lesbians and gays is a Black issue, because thousands of lesbians and gay men are Black. There is no hierarchy of oppression (Lorde, 1983, pp. 306–307).

Like Audre Lorde, Auntie Léa believed there was no hierarchy of oppression, worked on a number of social issues at once and addressed the different layers of oppression in each struggle. For example, one of the first issues Auntie Léa confronted as a union activist in the 1930s was sexual harassment – decades before the MeToo movement against sexual violence began in the mid-2000s.[4] In 1937, she brought up the issue of sexual harassment as a key grievance of the women workers during the labour strike of the garment workers. After the strike, as a Grievance Officer for the International Ladies' Garment Workers Union, she confronted the racism of the garment industry owners. In Chapters 4 and 5, I share stories about Auntie Léa's intersectional activism around workers' rights, sexism, and racism in the 1930s and 1940s.

In researching and writing this biography of Auntie Léa's life and intersectional activism, I have focused on moments that illustrate her ability to cross borders and build bridges between Montreal's Yiddish, French, and English-speaking communities. I have also focused on moments that show how Auntie Léa's social justice work was characterized by activist community care. My interest in writing about inter-community connection and activist care is grounded in my desire to share how crossing borders and practices of care are a continuing important force in social justice advocacy.

Border crossing

The practice of border crossing is often traced to the writing of Gloria Anzaldúa (1942–2004), who was a scholar of (American) Chicana cultural theory, feminist theory, and queer theory. Self-described as a "queer Chicana Tejana feminist patlache poet, fictionist, and cultural theorist" (Trujillo, 1997), Anzaldúa was interested in analysing the everyday experiences of people who, like herself, straddled and crossed borders of race, ethnicity, language, gender, sexuality, and geography (Anzaldúa, 2018).

Like Anzaldúa, psychologist Maria Root is interested in the ways people living in multilingual, multicultural, and multiracial families and communities cross borders. Root's (1996) research provides examples of the different ways people choose to border cross. Some people "bridge" linguistic, cultural, racial, and national borders by creating meaningful connections in two or more communities and by moving back and forth between them. Others camp out or put down roots in one community for extended periods of time and make their way into other camps from time to time. Alternatively, some people sit on the border between communities and use their experiences on that border as a central reference point for living their lives. Others foreground particular identities and background others in different situations or contexts. Some people choose to make use of more than one of these border crossing practices.

Auntie Léa never chose to put down roots in just one community. Instead, she made use of the three other practices Root describes to create inter-community connection, solidarity and care. I discuss Auntie Léa's practices of border crossing throughout the biography and describe the ways they allowed her to build bridges between diverse communities.

Activist community care

While Auntie Léa's activism took place in the streets and union halls, my own activist work has taken place in classrooms and the theatre. My teaching and research work as a professor at the University of Toronto, and my playwriting and theatre work as the Founder and Artistic Director of Gailey Road Productions, have focused on equity and justice in education, particularly around contemporary queer and trans activism in schools. Recently I have also engaged in archival research around queer and trans academic and community activism between the late 1940s and 1980s.[5] Many of the activist conversations I have participated in about queer and trans activism have made use of the concept of activist community care.

Activist community care practices are different from traditional individual practices of care work often carried out by women. Built on the ideas put forward by queer women of colour in the 1980s and 1990s (e.g., hooks, 2000; Lorde, 1983/2021; Moraga and Anzaldúa, 1981/2015), activist community care practices operate in the absence of institutional support – for example, the absence of healthcare support (Fink, 2021; Owis, 2024; Piepzna-Samarasinha, 2018). Working within networks found within their own communities, activists find ways of providing people with the resources they need without casting judgement or causing shame (Malatino, 2020).

Auntie Léa's social justice work included practices of activist community care. For example, in the 1930s and 1940s, she provided young women workers dealing with unwanted pregnancies with referrals to doctors for safer abortions. She also supported young women who chose to pursue their pregnancies in challenging circumstances. This care work was not part of her mandate as a union grievance officer. Auntie Léa chose to care for the women who came to her for help as part of her activist work.

Sources used in writing the biography
Archival research

My research for this biography began in January 2024 when I read through a great deal of the archival materials in Auntie Léa's dossier at the Jewish Public Library in Montreal. While I grew up in Montreal, I currently live in Toronto. During my visit to the library, I worked with community archivist Sam Pappas and collected both French and English interviews with Auntie Léa. Some of the interviews were audio-recorded; others were published in newspaper and magazine articles. Most of the interviews were undertaken in French and needed to be translated into English. I used the artificial intelligence program ChatGPT 4.0 to translate the French interview excerpts I've shared in this biography.

This is the first biography of Auntie Léa that has been written and published in English. There are, however, two superb biographical projects that have been undertaken in French. The first is a set of interviews undertaken in the 1980s by Quebec sociologist and activist Nicole Lacelle. They have been published alongside another set of interviews with union organizer Madeleine Parent, a friend and colleague of Auntie Léa's, in Lacelle's book *Entretiens avec Madeleine Parent et Léa Roback. Entretiens* was first published in 1988 and then reprinted in a second edition in 2005. My citations come from the second edition.

The second French biography project is a documentary film by Quebec filmmaker and activist Sophie Bissonnette, which was filmed in the late 1980s. *Des lumières dans la grande noirceur/ A vision in the darkness* premiered in 1991 and won the 1992 Cinema Award from the Office of Social Communications, the 1992 Sequences Award, and an honorary mention at the 1992 Golden Gate Awards in San Francisco.

The French title of Bissonnette's film *Des lumières dans la grande noirceur* can be literally translated into English as "The Lights in the Great Darkness." In Quebec, the period known as *la Grande Noirceur*/the Great Darkness refers to the 19 years Maurice Duplessis was premier of the province of Quebec (1936–1939, 1944–1959). The name captures the many oppressive laws and policies Duplessis put into place during his time as premier. It also captures the ways many of the people in Quebec struggled during the years he was in power. The "lights" in the Great Darkness were activists like my Auntie Léa who protested and fought against many of the oppressive laws and policies that characterized the Duplessis government.

I saw Sophie Bissonnette's film *Des lumières dans la grande noirceur/A vision in the darkness* at two film festivals in 1991: one in Toronto and one in Quebec City. For the Quebec City screening, I travelled with my Auntie Léa and Sophie Bissonnette from Montreal to Quebec City. We took the bus. Before the screening, we were invited to lunch by my great-aunt Annie Pedvis who lived in Quebec City. Auntie Annie wanted to celebrate Bissonnette and Auntie Léa's achievement. "We're proud of you," Auntie Annie told Auntie Léa.

Des lumières dans la grande noirceur has been made available with English subtitles for free by La Cinémathèque Québécoise.[6] Auntie Léa's stories about her life of activism are as compelling today as they were 35 years ago. I have included excerpts from Bissonnette's documentary film in this biography, using the English subtitles. In 2023, Sophie Bissonnette worked with historian Denyse Baillargeon to create a dossier of additional interview material that was not included in the film. The dossier is available in both French and English on a website created by La Cinémathèque Québécoise. English transcripts of the interviews, created by a professional translator, are available on the English website. I have used these translations when quoting from the additional interview material in the dossier.

During my first archival visit to the Jewish Public Library archives in January 2024, I had the opportunity to have dinner with Sophie Bissonnette and talk to her about this biography project. We discussed the way Sophie used the stories Auntie Léa shared with her to discuss the history of the activism of working-class urban women in Montreal. This was the perspective she took when she interviewed Auntie Léa and edited the interviews into a compelling documentary. Bissonnette encouraged me to find and articulate my own reasons for wanting to share stories about Auntie Léa's activist life and work. I have three.

The first, mentioned earlier, has to do with my desire to discuss the importance of building bridges and crossing borders in activism work. Today, we live in a political moment that has produced polarized views around human rights issues and a lack of dialogue. Auntie Léa's ability to cross linguistic, religious, cultural and class borders to advocate for workers' and women's rights makes a significant contribution to current conversations around human rights, equity, activism and education. Auntie Léa's particular gifts for border crossing and providing activist community care thread themselves through each of the chapters of the book. They provide me with a perspective for sharing stories of Auntie Léa's life and activism.

My second reason for writing this biography has to do with wanting to share the stories of Auntie Léa's life and work with English-speaking audiences. Because most of the interviews and biography projects that feature Auntie Léa's work are in French, many activists, university students, and educators in English-speaking Canada (and elsewhere) have never heard Auntie Léa talk about how she and others fought for workers' rights and for women's rights for seven decades in the twentieth century. I hope this biography will provide an opportunity for them to do so. I also hope it provides them with a preliminary understanding of Quebec and Canada's complex political and gender history in the twentieth century.

Finally, I decided to write this biography to honour Auntie Léa's desire to share stories of her activism with future generations of activists and educators. At the Quebec City premiere of *Des lumières dans la grande noirceur/A vision in the darkness* I remember someone in the audience asking Auntie Léa why she had agreed to participate in Bissonnette's documentary film. Auntie

Léa said she wanted young people to know about the activist achievements that took place even in the most repressive of political times. If stories about Auntie Léa's lifelong activism could help the next generation learn about these achievements, she wanted to support Bissonnette's project. Twenty-five years after Bissonnette's film first came out, I believe stories about Auntie Léa's life and activism have the power to both educate and inspire readers in English Canada.

Auntie Léa loved reading and had a strong belief in the importance of education. This is something we share. I have worked as a professor at the University of Toronto for over 30 years conducting research and educating university students, mostly new teachers, about pursuing equity in schools. I'm excited about sharing stories about Auntie Léa's activist life and work with other educators, students, and community activists.

During my first archival research visit to Montreal, I also spent time with Melanie Leavitt, who took me on a private walking tour about the Jewish left movement, focusing on the work Auntie Léa accomplished in the 1930s and 1940s. Sam Pappas, the community archivist at the Jewish Public Library, joined us. After the tour, we went for coffee, and Melanie told us the story of how she first met Auntie Léa. Melanie was introduced to her cousin Léa at a family bar mitzvah when she was 7 years old.[7] She had heard about Auntie Léa's activism from her mother Barbara Leavitt, and when she was introduced to Léa, Melanie told her that she wanted to become an activist as well.

> *"Mais, c'est formidable!,"* said Auntie Léa. "Well, that's fantastic!"

Melanie has become the activist she wanted to be and is currently working on a variety of public history projects that explore labour and women's history, including the walking tours and Jewish Public Library *recollections* podcast project discussed in this chapter. Melanie is also a board member of Mile End Memories, a socially engaged historical society in Montreal, and has recently joined the Board of Directors of the Léa Roback Foundation, which provides scholarships to socially committed women in financial need who are active and engaged in their communities. The Foundation as well as other honours Auntie Léa has received are discussed in Chapter 6.

Historical writing and podcasts

To contextualize the life stories Auntie Léa tells in her interviews with Sophie Bissonnette, Nicole Lacelle, and others, I consulted several pieces of historical writing about the times Auntie Léa lived and worked in. The insights of historians and writers Pierre Anctil, Naomi Klein, Merrily Weisbord, and others appear in the biography and provide important background knowledge about the historical contexts that produced the moments of activism and care Auntie Léa shares in her interviews. They also provide readers with an understanding of the antisemitism Auntie Léa faced as a Jewish child, worker, and activist living in Quebec in the twentieth century. Discussions of the ways Auntie Léa faced and challenged antisemitism are included throughout the biography.

As mentioned earlier, I also listened to a podcast called *recollections* produced by the Jewish Public Library which traces the history of Jewish left activism in Montreal in the

1930s and 1940s. Episode 3 of the podcast is called "Labour of Love" and it shares stories about union activism. Auntie Léa's union work is featured in the podcast through interviews with Melanie Leavitt and other Montreal and Quebec historians. Many of Leavitt's insights on Auntie Léa's life and activism shared in the podcast appear in this first chapter of the biography.

As I began to read a variety of historical material to provide me with a deeper understanding of the times Auntie Léa lived in, I found stories of queer and trans history, activism and care that were connected to moments in Auntie Léa's life and work. Some of these stories were new to me; others I had heard before. However, because generally, so much of queer and trans history, activism, and care is still unknown, I have included a number of these stories alongside stories about Auntie Léa. In sharing these queer and trans stories, I am working to cross a historical border between cisheteronormative[8] activist histories and queer and trans activist histories in the twentieth century.

In closing this introductory chapter of Auntie Léa's activist life and work, I turn to an interview she did at the age of 93. Towards the end of the interview, journalist Ghila Bénesty-Sroka asked Auntie Léa about her choice to lead a life of activism rather than build a professional career. Auntie Léa responded:

> What I loved was working with people. I loved them very much, I felt close to them. I told myself: "What am I going to do there, at the university?" I had already obtained a bachelor's degree in literature in Europe. It was not my style to make a career or to study for a long time and

then tell people what they had to do (Bénesty-Sroka, 1996, p. 83).

Auntie Léa's love of working with people shines through this biography. I know you will enjoy meeting her and reading about the many different ways she fought to make life better for the people she worked with.

2
Beauport and Montreal

Family and community life (1905–1929)

> Mama, who spoke good French like my father, always told us, "When they shout 'Damned Jews!' at you, respond, 'Why do you say that? Do we call you damned French Canadians?'" People didn't know what to retort and would leave.
>
> – Léa Roback[9]

***

My great-great-grandparents Isaac and Libby Roback immigrated to Canada from Poland around 1889. In the film *Des lumières dans la grande noirceur,* Auntie Léa tells Sophie Bissonnette the story of how the family came to Canada.

> In Poland my [paternal] grandparents had a shop, my grandmother ran it. Grandpa worked the farm. There was a Mr. Kleinberg. And he … made a living recruiting pedlars… immigrants. One day he was watching my grandpa work. He said, "Wouldn't you like to get out of farming?

> We'll take you to Quebec, to Canada (*Des lumières dans la grande noirceur,* 1991).

Isaac and Libby's immigration story is an illustration of a particular political and economic moment in Canada. They were invited to immigrate to Canada under John A. MacDonald's National Policy, which encouraged immigration from Eastern Europe. As Canadian historian Pierre Anctil explains:

> With a territory that was oversized in relation to its population of four million (in 1880), Canada could not afford to wait decades for natural population growth to meet its pressing manpower needs. In order to create a genuine domestic market and increase the number of taxpayers, MacDonald had no other option than to bring in a large number of people from elsewhere who could make a substantial contribution to the progress of the country (Anctil and Woodsworth, 2021, p. 64).

Like many other Eastern European Jewish immigrants at the time, Isaac and Libby Roback settled in Montreal which was the largest city in the country and the city in which industrialization was most advanced. In Montreal, there were a large number of opportunities for unskilled workers (Anctil and Woodsworth, 2021, p. 62). Isaac became a cutter in the men's clothing industry. His son Moses – Moishe – was apprenticing to become a cutter as well. But those plans changed after he married Fanny Steinhouse.

The marriage between my great-grandparents Moishe Roback and Fanny Steinhouse was arranged by a matchmaker when Fanny was only 16 years old. Auntie Léa explains:

> Mama was so pretty that my grandmother, Sarah, was afraid she might be sexually assaulted, so she wanted to find her a husband very quickly. Mama was married at 16, furious because she did not want to be tied down so soon. When I asked her why she didn't protest, she replied, "But those were not things we said to our parents!" My father was 13 years older than her. This was common at that time (Bénesty-Sroka, 1996, p. 81).

Auntie Léa's maternal grandparents, Berel and Sarah Steinhouse, had a different immigration story from that of Isaac and Libby Roback. Berel Steinhouse decided to leave Poland after getting into trouble because he refused to take off his hat in front of a portrait of Tsar Nicholas in a post office near Warsaw. Although Sarah understood political oppression and violence against Jews were increasing in Poland, she wasn't sure if she wanted to follow Berel to North America and asked their rabbi what to do. The rabbi told her to put a nail in water for a certain number of days, and if the water turned brown, it meant she should go. Of course, the nail rusted, and the water turned brown, so Sarah left with Berel to start a life in Canada.

Fanny and Moishe began their married life in Montreal on Guilbault Street, near Saint Laurent Boulevard in the heart of what was then Jewish Montreal, but moved to the rural town of Beauport when Auntie Léa was very small. The move to Beauport was financed by Fanny's parents, who borrowed money from the parish in Montmorency, Quebec, to provide Fanny and Moishe the money they needed to run a small general store in Beauport. Auntie Léa was the second of nine children. Harry was the first, Annie was the third, and my grandmother Rose was the fourth.

Following my grandmother were Lottie, Rebecca, Joe, Michael, and Leo. Their house "wasn't big, not even the kitchen," she told journalist Susan Schwartz. "Two of us slept in one bed in one room, and a third and fourth in the other bed. The living room was also a bedroom" (Schwartz and Roback, 1996/1997, p. 3).

Jewish life in Beauport

Moishe Roback was religious. Although he spent his days running the family's general store, what he enjoyed most was spending time studying the Torah and the Talmud.[10] Beauport didn't have a synagogue or an established Jewish community, so Moishe, who wanted his children to learn about their Jewish heritage and traditions, brought a rabbi into their home to teach Auntie Léa and her brothers and sisters about the Jewish holidays. On Saturdays, Moishe would walk eight and a half kilometres from his home in Beauport to the synagogue in Quebec City with his eldest son, Harry, Auntie Léa's older brother.[11] For major Jewish holidays, Fanny and the rest of the children would also go to Quebec City and spend the night somewhere near the synagogue so they didn't have to walk back and forth between Beauport and Quebec City each day.

Moishe not only loved reading Torah, he loved reading in general. Auntie Léa told us that when Fanny sent him to Quebec City to buy kosher meat, he often forgot to bring back what she had asked for. But he always returned with a book in his pocket. For Moishe, buying books was more important than buying meat for dinner. Both Moishe and Fanny wanted their children to know how to read and write Yiddish. Moishe would read Yiddish stories to them – stories by Jewish writers like Sholem Aleichem, whose tale *Tevye the Dairyman and His Daughters* about Jewish life in Russia was used to write the book for the 1964 Broadway musical *A Fiddler on the Roof.*

Fanny and Moishe raised their children to understand the importance of helping others and taught them to live by the saying, "We must do something!" In an interview with Sophie Bissonnette, Auntie Léa told her:

> The saying's still used all the time. "We must do something." That's it. Passed from father to son all the way along. Still today (*Des lumières dans la grande noirceur*, 1991).

When Bissonnette asked Auntie Léa if the saying "We must do something" inspired her politically, Auntie Léa answered:

> Sure, it did. Of course. It was the way we were brought up. It inspired me. For me charity wasn't... write a check, finished. At home it wasn't like that, you must do something (*Des lumières dans la grande noirceur*, 1991).

Caring for the sick and supporting people who were hungry or needed shelter was simply what you did in Auntie Léa's family. "That's my religion," she explained to the curator who interviewed her in 1996 for an exhibit on immigrants that was about to open at the *Musée de la civilisation* in Quebec City. "Knowing how to live, not only for yourself but also for others, who need help" (Schwartz and Roback, 1996/1997, p. 5).

Auntie Léa and her siblings were the only Jewish family living in Beauport. Dealing with antisemitism and people who made antisemitic remarks was part of their everyday life. For example, the local priest, who had never met any Jews before the Robacks arrived in Beauport, told his parishioners, "You should not buy from Jews, but rather support Mr. Roy, who is a Catholic, a French Canadian" (Bénesty-Sroka, 1996, p. 81).

In her film, Sophie Bissonnette illustrated this moment when she read aloud a newspaper article from a Montreal Yiddish daily newspaper that had been published at the time. The article from the *Keneder Aldler/The Jewish Daily Eagle* stated:

> In Beauport, there's a Jewish shopkeeper [Moishe Roback] respected by the villagers. It's shocking that a priest could use his influence to try to chase him from his home for 4 years. During a mass at the church the priest strictly forbad anyone to sell a store to a Jew (*Des lumières dans la grande noirceur,* 1991).

Auntie Léa herself discussed the moment in the following way:

> When they came, Dad… He was marvelous. He held his ground. He said, "I have as much right as you. And I'm making an honest living. People here support us." Mom and Dad gave credit. Half the time it wasn't paid back. Dad would say, "What can I take? The kids? We have enough already." That was that (*Des lumières dans la grande noirceur,* 1991).

Pierre Anctil explains that the antisemitism the Roback family faced in the early 1900s was brought to Canada and Quebec from Europe. It first emerged in Germany in the late nineteenth century and was then taken up in France and Great Britain, countries that were close to Canada, economically and politically. Antisemitism, which can be defined as prejudice against Jews or the hatred of Jews, circulated in English-language Protestant communities differently than it circulated in French-language Catholic communities.

In French-speaking communities, antisemitism circulated through the teachings of the Catholic Church, in local parishes, by local priests, like the priest in Beauport who told his parishioners not to buy goods from Jews. Historian Pierre Anctil explains,

> Before the Vatican Council of the 60s [1960s], the Catholic Church was the main vehicle for hostility to Jews. French Canadians went to mass. They absorbed antisemitism in the liturgy, in the teachings, in the preaching. And often we find, um, that when Jews would say, well, this, sorry, this is antisemitic. And the French Canadians would answer, no, it's not. We're not antisemites, we just repeat what the priests say. We just repeat what our masters or our forebears say.
>
> If the church says it, it can't be wrong. See, that was the problem. The objections of the church were doctrinal. In other words, a Jewish person is someone that rejected Christ and is not likely to be a good citizen, a good person, to be welcomed in the Catholic environment.
>
> The British said something else. They said, for racial reasons, we should reject [Jews]. This is more the German version [of antisemitism]. For racial reasons, we should reject Jews because they contaminate our people. French Canadians didn't say this because the notion of the Church is that all humanity can be converted to Catholicism, and these racial barriers are more superficial (Jewish Public Library, 2024, *recollections*, Episode 1).

Anctil further explains that the British believed in assimilation: the quicker Eastern European Jews could learn English and become good Protestants, the better it would be for them and for the Jewish community altogether. This was the reason why the English-language Protestant school boards in Montreal and Quebec City accepted Jewish children like the Roback children into their schools, and why Auntie Léa and her siblings took the train to Quebec City to attend a Protestant school.

As the opening quote to this chapter reveals, Fanny Roback taught her children to respond to their neighbours' antisemitic slurs – slurs like "damned Jew" – with a question: "Why do you say that? Do we call you damned French Canadians?" Gradually people in Beauport stopped calling the Roback children names, and they were able to make friends with the other children who lived nearby (Bénesty-Sroka, 1996, p. 81). These friendships were an early example of the way Auntie Léa crossed linguistic and religious borders to connect with her Catholic French-Canadian neighbours. Her mother Fanny connected with their neighbours by raising a large family. "You're Jewish," Auntie Léa recalled them saying. "But you're all right, Mrs. Roback. You have a baby every year, just like us" (Schwartz and Roback, 1996/1997, p. 6).

Auntie Léa never internalized the antisemitism she experienced as a child or adult. She always felt proud to be Jewish. When she was asked by French Canadian interviewers if she was Polish, Auntie Léa would always respond, "No, I am Jewish and my parents came from Poland" (Harris and Roback, 1988). She wanted to set the record straight. It was important for Auntie Léa that French Canadian journalists know she was Jewish. If they thought her work was important enough to write about, then they needed to know that they were writing about the work of a Jewish activist.

When journalist Ghila Bénesty-Sroka asked Auntie Léa if she had ever faced antisemitic remarks or ideas within the Quebec feminist movement, Auntie Léa answered, "People don't like Jews." When asked if she meant people in Quebec, Auntie Léa clarified, "Everywhere!" Then she explained:

> It will take more than you, more than me to make up for lost time, to get the prejudices that have been instilled in people's heads out. Some of my Francophone friends are very nice, but they still have a lot of prejudices against Jews ... It's long and difficult to eliminate the effects of this poison that has been distilled for decades in schools, by religion (Bénesty-Sroka, 1996, p. 85).

In her lifelong fight against antisemitism (in addition to her fights for workers' and women's rights and against racism), Auntie Léa developed strategies to deal with the antisemitic remarks she heard. She'd respond, "The God you pray to in your Catholic religion was a Jew!" Antisemitic remarks always made Auntie Léa angry, but she learned that there was an art to expressing her anger. "Mama always said if you get angry with a smile, people understand more quickly" (Bénesty-Sroka, 1996, p. 82).

On antisemitism: Then and now

Like historian Pierre Anctil, writer and activist Naomi Klein has also researched the history of antisemitism. Writing about responses to antisemitism in the first decades of the twentieth century, Klein reports that Jewish intellectual life in both Europe and North America "roared with drag-down debates over what was then euphemistically called 'the Jewish Question'" (Klein, 2023, p. 290). Debates about the Jewish Question included discussions about how to challenge antisemitism in both Europe and North America, the role cultural assimilation might play in challenging antisemitism, and the possibilities and dangers of Zionism. Klein writes:

> Should Jews strive for full equality in Christian societies – voting rights, access to all industries (the position of the Social Democrats)? Or should the goal be revolutionary transformation of those societies accompanied by full Jewish assimilation into the liberated proletariat since religion would be less necessary as a source of solace ("Religion is the sight of the oppressed creature, the heart of a heartless world, and the soul of the soulless conditions. It is the opium of the people," Marx wrote …)? Was Judaism a prison from which the revolution would offer liberation (as the Bolsheviks claimed, though many conceded that there was a need to protect the right to religious practice in private life)? Or was Jewish assimilation, even in a socialist society, a trap eliding the need for European Jews' distinct culture and language to be protected within a multiethnic, multinational workers' society (the Bund's "hereness" position)? Or was Jew-hatred simply too deep on the continent, too primal, for any of this to work, so that Jewish liberation could be found only in the working-class movements of the amnesiac Americas (the position held by many of my family members as they crossed the Atlantic)? Or was even that mere fantasy, especially under the harsh, overtly racist, and anti-Semitic immigration laws introduced by the United States and Canada in the 1920s and '30s, making the only hope for Jewish safety a nation-state of their own, where wandering would end and socialism could become a reality (the view of the Labour Zionists) (Klein, 2023, p. 291).

Simply put, archivist Eddie Paul from the Jewish Public Library in Montreal says this: While the Bundists believed in the idea of "hereness" – building a home wherever Jews lived – the Zionists believed in "thereness" – building a home in Palestine where all Jews would live once a Jewish state was created (Jewish Public Library, 2024b, *recollections*, Episode 2). Unlike the Zionists, Bundists believed Jews would only be free when everyone was free, and not in building, as Klein puts it, "a militarized ghetto on Palestinian land" (Klein, 2023, p. 291).

In her interview with Auntie Léa, Nicole Lacelle asked if the Roback family had been interested in Zionism. Auntie Léa responded no. She remembered that her father was once approached about becoming a Zionist in 1913, but her father wasn't interested. "In our family," she said, "it just didn't resonate." When Lacelle asked her why, Auntie Léa said:

> Maybe partly because Herzl's idea, the founder's notion, that Jews needed a country to be respected, didn't align with our experience. In Beauport, when I was little, we were the only Jewish family, and we were respected— well, after we made them understand that we were human beings like them and had the same rights … There are good people everywhere and scoundrels everywhere. Zionism just wasn't part of our way of life … However, I want to emphasize that we were very proud of our culture. We didn't allow anyone to say "damn Jew" or claim that Jews were like this or that, in any language (Lacelle and Roback, 2005, pp. 168–169).

The debate over the Jewish Question ended in the 1930s and 1940s, when the Nazis began to annihilate Jews in the European countries they gained control of, and the United States and Canada refused to accept European Jewish refugees into their countries.[12] As Klein puts it, "the whole terrain on which the debate was happening was crushed by terror, betrayal and abandonment" (Klein, 2023, p. 292).

Known today as the Holocaust, the systematic, state-sponsored persecution and murder of six million European Jews by the Nazi German regime and its allies and collaborators was an evolving process that took place throughout Europe between 1933 and 1945 (United States Holocaust Memorial Museum, 2021). The Nazi regime also persecuted and murdered millions of other victims, including Black people in Germany; civilians (non-Jewish) accused of disobedience, resistance or partisan activity; gay men, bisexual men, or men accused of homosexuality in Germany; Jehovah's Witnesses; people with disabilities; Poles; political opponents and dissenters in Germany; Roma people; social outsiders in Germany derogatorily labelled as "asocials" and "professional criminals"; and Soviet prisoners of war.

The Nazi persecution of Jews became increasingly radical between 1933 and 1945 and culminated in a plan that was called "The Final Solution to the Jewish Question." The "Final Solution" was the organized and systematic mass murder of European Jews. The Nazi German regime implemented this genocide between 1941 and 1945 (United States Holocaust Memorial Museum, 2021). After the Holocaust Klein argues, there was only one answer to the Jewish Question that asserted itself with any great confidence: Zionism (Klein, 2023, p. 295).

The Holocaust was fuelled by antisemitism which was a basic tenet of Nazi ideology. While the Nazis promoted and practiced a particularly virulent form of antisemitism, the Nazis did not invent antisemitism; it is an old and widespread prejudice that has taken many forms throughout European history. In the Middle Ages (500–1400) prejudices against Jews were primarily based in early Christian myths that Jews were responsible for the death of Jesus Christ. Religious prejudices continued in early modern Europe (1400–1800), when Jews were excluded from most aspects of economic, social, and political life. This exclusion contributed to stereotypes of Jews as outsiders. As Europe became more secular, many legal restrictions on Jews were lifted, but new forms of antisemitism established themselves in the eighteenth and nineteenth centuries: economic, nationalist, and racial antisemitism. Jews were believed to be responsible for a variety of social and political crises in European industrial societies. New theories of race, eugenics, and Social Darwinism falsely justified these beliefs. Nazi ideology drew upon all of these forms of antisemitism, but especially racial antisemitism, and the idea that Jews were a separate and inferior race that needed to be removed from German society (United States Holocaust Memorial Museum, 2022b).

Reflecting on her research into the history of Jewish hatred, Klein writes that she is struck by how contradictory stereotypes and conspiracy theories about Jews have been over the centuries, and in particular in Nazi Germany:

> Are Jews greedy bankers scheming to get Christian property so we can pocket the money? Or are we rabble-rousing communists scheming to do away with capitalism altogether? A widely-circulated Nazi caricature depicts the "eternal Jew" – a hunched man with gold coins in one hand and a map of Germany with a

hammer and sickle on it in the other, somehow managing to be an arch capitalist and a revolutionary Marxist at the same time. Conspiracy theories don't require internal consistency to find traction … Still it's striking that the two most tenacious lines of attack that Jews have faced over the generations – the scheming Jewish bankers and the scheming Jewish Marxists – are perennially on a logical collision course with each other (Klein, 2023, p. 288).

It's been more than 100 years since the local priest in Beauport told his parishioners not to buy goods from the Roback family so they could not "pocket the money" at the expense of Catholic French Canadians. And it's been several decades since Auntie Léa told Ghila Bénesty-Sroka it would take a long time to eliminate the poison of antisemitism. Auntie Léa was right. Jewish communities in North America continue to be targeted by antisemitic violence: In 2018, eleven congregants were murdered at the Tree of Life Synagogue in Pittsburgh. In 2019, there were shootings at a Chabad synagogue in Poway, California. And on 6 January 2021, at the United States Capitol insurrection in Washington, D.C., there were displays of Nazi symbols. In Canada, during the summer of 2024, antisemitic graffiti was painted on the walls of Canadian Jewish synagogues, and bomb threats were made to Jewish congregations across the country (Logan, 2024).

In response to ongoing antisemitic violence in the United States and Canada, the organization Jewish Voice for Peace believes that antisemitism needs to be fought "within, and as part of, other struggles against oppression and for collective liberation."

Echoing the Bundists' belief in "hereness" they write, "Our safety is bound together with the safety of all people, and none of us is free if we aren't all free" (Jewish Voice for Peace, 2023).

Currently, Jewish Voice for Peace is involved in responding to the ongoing military and political conflict between Israel and Palestine and issues around land and self-determination for the Palestinian people (Jewish Voice for Peace, 2024). Key aspects of the conflict include the Israeli occupation of the West Bank and Gaza Strip, Israeli settlements, borders, security, water rights, the permit regime, Palestinian freedom of movement, and the Palestinian right of return.[13] This work aligns with Auntie Léa's own thinking about justice for Palestinians. For example, when asked by Ghila Bénesty-Sroka about her position on "the Palestinian question," Auntie Léa answered:

> I try to put myself a little in the place of the Palestinians. If someone told me that I can't live in such and such a place, I would say damn it and go live where I have the means to do so. If I were Palestinian, I would fight for my rights and I would have the right to do so, just as the Israelis also have their rights (Bénesty-Sroka, 1996, p. 84).

Like other contemporary activists, both Jewish and non-Jewish, Auntie Léa wore a *keffiyeh* to demonstrate her support for the struggle of the Palestinian people.[14] As an anti-war activist, she would have been horrified by the current violence in Israel, Gaza, the West Bank, and Lebanon – violence perpetrated by Hamas, Hezbollah and the Israeli government. At the same time, Auntie Léa would have been disturbed and angry at the silence of leftist activists about current antisemitic violence committed against Jews in Europe and North America, such as the attacks on Israeli soccer fans in Amsterdam in November 2024 (Reuters, 2024). Further discussion of Auntie Léa's anti-war activism appears in Chapter 5.

From Beauport to Montreal

Auntie Léa's life in Beauport came to an end in 1919 when the Roback family returned to Montreal. Finding a place for a large Jewish family to live wasn't easy.

> … when you moved with a big family, it was hard. That and being Jewish. That was tough. He [our landlord] was a francophone, [and] didn't want a Jewish family. Didn't want children. But we got it. Mama convinced him. I think she told him a little white lie, that she only had three or four kids. Once we moved in [with nine children], well … (*Des lumières dans la grande noirceur,* 1991).

Around the same time Auntie Léa and her family moved back to Montreal, her grandparents, Berel and Sarah Steinhouse, were part of a movement to establish a Jewish home for the elderly. The first home was built in 1910, and the second was built in 1923. In honour of the work undertaken by the Steinhouse family and their financial contributions, the second home was named the B. & S. Steinhouse Old People's Home. In one of her interviews with Sophie Bissonnette, Auntie Léa tells the story of her grandparents' involvement like this:

> … my maternal grandparents, owned a furniture store. They lived comfortably. And my grandmother had heard that a Jewish family … that the old mother was sleeping on the balcony in November [when temperatures go as low as 0 degrees Celsius]. "My God, that's not possible! It's inhumane!" So grandmother said, "Bring her to my

house." My grandmother lived on Jeanne-Mance Street. And she let the woman sleep at her place until we could find her a family. And then my grandmother said to my grandfather (in Yiddish), *"Bero, besaf hobn a heim für die jüdische Älter* [Bero, we need a home for Jewish seniors!]" And my grandfather said, "But that would cost a fortune!" And she said, "Too bad!" [Inaudible.] She had a little bag [for the money she could save], and each time she put a little more money aside, my mother made her a slightly bigger bag to put [her money in] . . . and one day she said to my grandfather (in Yiddish), *"Bero, ikh hob die Geld* [Bero, I have the money!]" (A Jewish Seniors' Residence Founded by Her Grandmother, 2023).

As she had been taught, and then as she taught her own children, Sarah Steinhouse was moved to "do something" to support the well-being of the elderly. It was an act of activism and care, and an example of the role Jewish women in Montreal have had in building up social service and health institutions for their communities. Over the decades, the B. & S. Steinhouse Old People's Home moved north and west to the Jewish suburb of Côte Saint-Luc and was renamed the Maimonides Hospital and Home for the Aged. The name was chosen to honour Rabbi Moshe Bar Maimon, who was also known as Maimonides. Maimonides was an important rabbi, philosopher, and doctor in Jewish history. When I was growing up in the 1960s and 1970s, my grandmother, Rose Roback Goldstein, carried on the Steinhouse family commitment to the hospital and home by volunteering at the Maimonides Gift Shop. Rose was much loved by the staff of Maimonides and by visitors who came to the gift shop, and I have vivid memories of visiting her there and listening to her chat with everyone who walked in.

In the late sixties, when I was in grade 6, the cleaning staff at Maimonides went on strike. The strike was still going on during my Easter holiday break from school, and my grandmother asked me if I would volunteer to help the staff who were not on strike keep their wards clean. Knowing that Auntie Léa would not approve of me crossing the picket line, I told my grandmother I was worried that Auntie Léa would call me a "scab" (a strikebreaker). My grandmother told me that Auntie Léa would never call me a scab, and I shouldn't let that stand in the way of volunteering when my help was needed. Like Auntie Léa and my grandmother, I had been raised to live by the saying "We must do something!" so I spent some of my Easter holiday break cleaning toilets at Maimonides with my best friend Sandy Zakuta. Although I don't remember my Auntie Léa and my grandmother fighting about us crossing the picket line during the strike at Maimonides (at least not in front of me), I know that at times their politics were not always compatible. I do, however, remember feeling very uncomfortable crossing the picket lines at Maimonides, and ever since then I've made it a point not to cross one.

His Majesty's theatre and Lucien Lacouture

As discussed in Chapter 1, Auntie Léa's first job in Montreal was working as a receptionist at British American Dyeworks. In 1922, she left the job and began working as a cashier in the box office at His Majesty's Theatre. She found the job through a customer who brought something in to be cleaned.

> One day this tiny woman came in. I'll never forget her, Miss Taft. She brought something in for cleaning. She worked as a cashier at the theatre. A theatre, not a movie house. She watched me working and said, "Why work with rich people's laundry? Come work at the theatre." Me, who adored the theatre. My God. I'd have done anything to go. And I did go! So, I worked at His Majesty's [Theatre] (*Des lumières dans la grande noirceur*, 1991).

Auntie Léa met all kinds of people while working at His Majesty's Theatre. One of them was fashion designer Lucien Lacouture who designed clothes for affluent, "high society" women in Montreal during the 1920s and early 1930s (McCord Stewart Museum, 2019). Lacouture was born in Sorel, Quebec, in 1895, and studied at the Fashion Academy in New York. He returned to Montreal in 1926, where he opened his own atelier and lived as an out gay man at a time when homosexuality was illegal (McCord Stewart Museum, 2019). Lacouture befriended Auntie Léa and invited her to his home where she met other gay men and artists. "We'd visit, discuss books," Auntie Léa told Sophie Bissonnette. "They read a lot. They had wonderful records. The best music. The three "B"s [Bach, Beethoven, and Brahms], Schubert and all. We'd sip a good glass of wine. They were great cooks, knew how to sew." Auntie Léa loved spending time with Lacouture and his friends and could have "lived that life forever" (*Des lumières dans la grande noirceur*, 1991).

Influenced by the time she spent with Lucien Lacouture, Auntie Léa always appreciated well-made, beautifully designed clothes, and when she had the opportunity, she wore beautiful clothes herself. For example, in a photo taken in the 1920s, Auntie Léa is wearing a stylish sweater and skirt set with a fashionable cloche hat on her head and a fur stole around her shoulders. When I started looking for images of the kinds of clothing Lucien Lacouture designed for his wealthy clientele, I came upon an image of a cherry-red wool coat topped with a fur stole that is very similar to the kind of stole Auntie Léa had around her shoulders in the photograph. Wearing lovely clothes was another way Auntie Léa lived as a political free spirit, breaking stereotypes about how activists should dress and behave. Sometimes this worked against her, however. For example, when Auntie Léa wanted to join the Communist Party in Berlin, they were suspicious of her because of the clothes she was wearing. In an interview with Sophie Bissonnette, Auntie Léa explains:

> They wore suits, leather or faux leather jacket, red, the beret, and flat-heeled shoes … And me, Léa Roback, they didn't accept me like that, pronto! Oh no. Why? I had a coat, fur, real fur, beige fox. I had a boyish hat that was worn at that time, I had short hair. I had high-heeled shoes. The first time I arrived, I will never forget it. Never, never, never! Because either I was an informant or I was a loose woman … But in the end, they accepted me. They knew it was because I wanted to, because I wanted to get involved. And then, I got along very well with these comrades (*Joining The Communist Party in Berlin (1932)*, 2023).

Bohemian Montreal

Lucien Lacouture and his friends were part of a community which later became known as Bohemian Montreal. Lesbian writer and poet Elsa Gidlow who lived in Montreal before Auntie Léa returned to the city, was also friendly with Lacouture. In her 1986 autobiography *I Come With My Songs*, Gidlow writes that she was able to find her people in Bohemian Montreal – people, she could "enjoy, converse with, learn from, and perhaps love" (Gidlow, 1986, p. 72). She formed a close, lifelong friendship with writer Rosewell Mills, who, like Lucien Lacouture, was living his life as an openly gay man.

In an act of queer care, Mills took Gidlow under his wing and nicknamed her Sappho because she was a strong and independent poet like Sappho (Gidlow, 1986, pp. 72–75). While Gidlow kept the nickname in Montreal, when she moved to New York she asked Lucien Lacouture (who had also moved to New York to study at the Fashion Academy) not to call her Sappho anymore as the name belonged to her Montreal life (Gidlow, 1986, p. 131). In Montreal, Gidlow worked as a secretary at a shipping company, which didn't pay much. Mills bought Gidlow clothes and took her to plays and operas she couldn't afford on her salary. He also taught Gidlow about alternative cultures and queer history and introduced her to writers like Oscar Wilde and Charles Baudelaire whose "glamorous sinfulness and metaphysical retreat from middle-class living" impressed her and provided a way for her to think about how she might create her own life as a lesbian writer and poet (Gidlow, 1986, p. 71).

In 1917, Gidlow and Mills started a newspaper called *Les Mouches Fantastiques,* which contemporary Montreal researcher and writer Lucy Uprichard (2019) has described as a mixed anti-war and cultural criticism magazine. It featured editorials, poetry, and the writing of people Gidlow and Mills admired. *Les Mouches*

Fantastiques ran for five issues and became what Uprichard believes to be the first ever explicitly queer publication in North America. The final issue of *Les Mouches Fantastiques* was published in early 1920, a few months before Gidlow moved to New York, where she would write and publish *On A Grey Thread*, her first full-length collection and the very first book of lesbian poetry in North America (Uprichard, 2019). Elsa Gidlow lived a life as a lesbian feminist writer and poet decades before homosexuality was decriminalized and feminism had become part of public thinking. As Uprichard writes, "It took guts to be a woman like Elsa Gidlow" (Uprichard, 2019). Of course, the same can be said about Rosewell Mills and Lucien Lacouture.

Auntie Léa's friendship with Lucien Lacouture was important to her – so important that she almost lost her job as a youth worker at the Young Women's Hebrew Association (YWHA) over it. One of the wealthy women who bought clothes designed by Lacouture was on the Board of Directors running the YWHA. When the board member found out that Auntie Léa was friends with Lacouture, she was upset. Reflecting the homophobia of the era, she didn't think Auntie Léa should be friends with a gay man. As Auntie Léa explains:

> One fine day, [she] stopped by Lacouture's; he asked if she knew me, telling her I was a very good friend. So, she came to see me at the office, all upset despite her furs and her very elegant little hat [even her furs and hat didn't prevent her from being upset]: "Do you know Lucien Lacouture?" "Of course, he's one of my friends." "Do you know who he is?" I pretended not to understand, and said, "Well, he's a tailor." That's not what I mean.

> Do you know what he is?" "No, tell me." "He's not… like a man." "Really… it's true that he's very kind, cooks well, and loves beautiful music…" And she told me that as long as I worked there, I shouldn't associate with him (Lacelle and Roback, 2005, p. 132).

Auntie Léa had no intention of ending her friendship with Lacouture. She decided to speak to two women who volunteered in the Jewish community and ask them to speak to the board member who was upset. They agreed to do so and reminded the board member that Auntie Léa had been hired based on her abilities, not on who she associated with. The matter was dropped, but the story reveals the kind of discrimination gay men living in Montreal in the 1930s faced. When Lucien Lacouture died at the young age of 39, the evenings full of talk about books, music and wine that Auntie Léa loved so much came to an end. They did not last forever, as Auntie Léa had wished, but they did last for many years.

From Montreal to Grenoble

Another person Auntie Léa met while working at His Majesty's Theatre was an actor named Madame Dax. She was part of a touring French troupe from Paris and would end up playing an important role in Auntie Léa's life.

While she was working at the box office, Auntie Léa always had a book on hand to read when she wasn't busy. She particularly enjoyed reading French literature – Zola, or Proust, Anatole France, and all of the authors who were on the "Index" books that had been blacklisted or censored by the Church. Madame Dax would see Auntie Léa in the box office and ask her about the books she was reading. One day, when Auntie Léa was visiting Madame Dax in her dressing room, she asked Auntie Léa, "Why don't you go study in France? It's cheaper than here. In Grenoble, there's a very good Chair in literature" (Lacelle and Roback, 2005, pp. 114–115). Auntie Léa loved the idea and began saving for a one-way boat ticket to France and enough money to live on for a year.

When Auntie Léa left Montreal to study at the Université de Grenoble she knew she would need to find work once she arrived in France but wasn't worried about how this would happen. On the boat, she became friendly with three women. One was a woman from Spain who was travelling with a young American woman Auntie Léa's age, 22 years-old. The third woman was an older aunt, the *tia*, who was chaperoning them. These new acquaintances would end up changing how Auntie Léa began her first trip to Europe. As she told Nicole Lacelle:

> Maria had an American, English-speaking boyfriend who wanted to marry her, but at that time, marriage with a *gringo* was out of the question. So, they needed to get her out of that environment and go to Spain, where they had family. We were on the De Grasse, I'll always remember it. What fun we had on that boat! Once we arrived in Paris, the aunt asked me if I wanted to translate for her; she needed to buy a silver table service from a jeweller on Rue Rochechouart. She had the address and the name; I looked at the name and thought, "They must be Jews!" … So, we get to the shop, I start looking around, and then I drop a comment in Yiddish (Lacelle and Roback, 2005, p. 115).

Auntie Léa's (border-crossing) use of Yiddish piqued the jeweller's interest, and he asked her where she was from. When Auntie Léa told him she was from Canada, the jeweller couldn't believe she spoke Yiddish. Auntie Léa told him she came from a Jewish family that spoke Yiddish at home and established a connection with the jeweller based on their shared Jewishness. When *Tia* made her selection – some cutlery and a platter – the jeweller sold it to her at a very good price. *Tia* was so happy that she invited Auntie Léa to join them in Spain. Her classes in Grenoble didn't start until February, so Auntie Léa took the train with *Tia* and her family and went to Spain. She had a wonderful time.

> My goodness, I lived it, my dear; I lived it so deeply, I will never forget it, never. First, we went up Mount Tibidabo, in the mountains, to a small guesthouse ... Then we went down to Barcelona. For me, it was the first time, Lea Roback, from Beauport, was entering a house of "the super-rich." The wallpaper wasn't paper; it was brocade. Oh! It was marvelous, marvelous! The furniture, all carved, it was extraordinarily luxurious. But Maria, no matter what, refused to marry a Spaniard. So, they went back to America. Poor *Tia*, she cried so much; but the silverware calmed her down a bit—she always had her silverware. Maria, later on, ended up marrying her American, but I lost touch with her; I stayed in Grenoble. Then, in 1926, the franc dropped to two and a half cents! (Lacelle and Roback, 2005, pp. 116–117).

When Auntie Léa had calculated how much money she'd need to stay in Grenoble, she didn't expect the franc to drop as much as it did. She didn't have enough money to finish the degree she was enrolled in, so she went down to Nice to work. There she met two middle-class women from England who tried to speak French with Auntie Léa. When Auntie Léa decided to put them at ease by speaking to them in English, they asked her where she was from. When she said Canada, they exclaimed, "Oh, she belongs to us!" This shocked and angered Auntie Léa so much that from that moment on, she always told British tourists she was American. She hated the idea that the British thought Canada "belonged" to Britain. When Lacelle asked Auntie Léa if she was politically active in Grenoble, she said:

> No. There wasn't even a decent union; the glovemakers worked from home, in small shops. There was felt and fabric production, but the large manufacturers—brocade, wool—were in Lyon. It was very conservative, even royalist; there were royalists in Grenoble, three families. The main industry was tourism: skiing, the valley, and the beautiful mountains. No, I wasn't politically active at all there; I was studying (Lacelle and Roback, 2005, pp. 116–117).

From Grenoble to Montreal to New York City

When Auntie Léa discovered she didn't have enough money to finish her studies in Grenoble, she wrote to her grandfather Berel Steinhouse who sent her money to take a ship back to Montreal. Arriving back in Montreal was disappointing. Because of the censorship practices in Quebec, which were the result of the strong influence and control exerted by the Catholic church in partnership with the provincial government, there was no theatre, and all of the books Auntie Léa wanted to read were blacklisted. The Catholic church had created a list of books that it considered dangerous to the faith and morals of their parishioners and published the titles in a document entitled *Index Librorum Prohibitorum*, Index of Prohibited Books, often simply referred to as "the Index." Feeling limited by life under censorship, Auntie Léa left Montreal and went to New York, where she worked at a variety of jobs. In her interview with Nicole Lacelle, Auntie Léa talked about two of them. The first was a job as a salesperson in a women's clothing store. The second was a receptionist job at a law firm. She lost both those jobs, which didn't upset her at all as it gave her more free time to read.

> I lost [the first] job because I told a woman, "That's not a dress for you, it makes you look big. You need stripes, madam!" The manager overheard me and said, "You don't have to tell her how to dress, she wants a dress, sell it to her." We got into an argument, and she told me to take $4 from the cash register and never come back. I took my $4, I was happy, and I went to the library on the corner of 42nd Street and 5th Avenue. I had a fantastic afternoon.
>
> After that, I got a job at a law firm, near Wall Street. I was a receptionist; one day, the switchboard operator was out, and the lawyers asked me to take over. It was an old switchboard with dozens of cords! I had never done that in my life, so I said, "It's impossible, I've never done this." "Ah!" they explained, "you pull this and plug that, watch the red light, the green light, it's surely not complicated." So, I gave it a try. Unplugged everything, but one poor lawyer—I cut off his call; he came down

and yelled at me. I told him, "I told you I had never done this," but he gave me $15 and fired me. I was happy, I had my afternoon free, and I thought, "Hey, I'll write to Henri [Harry, her older brother]" (Lacelle and Roback, 2005, pp. 117–118).

It must have been a sad letter, Auntie Léa later told Sophie Bissonnette, because when Uncle Harry wrote back, he invited Auntie Léa to join him and his wife Betty in Berlin. Uncle Harry, who was called Harry in English and Henri in French, was studying medicine there and working in hospitals at night to pay the bills. Uncle Harry had decided to go to Berlin to study because the courses were very rigorous, and it was less expensive than attending medical school in Montreal or New York. "In Germany," Auntie Léa told Nicole Lacelle, "he could complete his entire medical degree for what it would have cost him for just one year at Columbia" (Lacelle and Roback, 2005, pp. 118). As well, there was a quota of Jewish students accepted into McGill University in Montreal, making admission to medical school difficult for Harry (Bénesty-Sroka, 1996, pp. 83).

In his letter to Auntie Léa, Uncle Harry said, "Find yourself $90, take the boat and come. I've got a room with a very kind lady in the old quarter of Berlin; we'll put a curtain between two small beds, we'll manage" (Lacelle and Roback, 2005, pp. 118).

Auntie Léa was thrilled to receive Uncle Harry's invitation. She asked her grandfather for enough money for a third-class ticket and got on a ship to Berlin. Her plans were to finish her university degree in Germany. It was 1929, and Auntie Léa was about to witness the impact of the Great Depression and the rise of

Nazism in Berlin. It would deepen her early understanding of the antisemitism she experienced growing up in Beauport and Montreal, and it would be the beginning of a political education that would inform the direction her life would take for the next 30 years.

3
Berlin and Montreal

Political learning and Communist Party work (1929–1958)

> "I learned a great deal. It was truly enriching … Fantastic years.
> Often hungry years, but you survive."
>
> – Léa Roback[15]

***

In 1929, at the age of 25, Auntie Léa returned to Europe to join her older brother Harry and his wife Betty in Berlin. When she arrived, she could only say, "Hello," *Guten Tag*. She enrolled in university again, learned German, explored Berlin and was introduced to German concerts, operettas, and workers' theatre: "It was wonderful, the workers' theatre!" Auntie Léa told Nicole Lacelle. "We, the students, always went to the rehearsals for one mark, which was maybe worth 25 cents" (Lacelle and Roback, 2005, p. 119). To earn money to survive, she taught English to "worried Jews" who were monitoring the rise of Hitler and antisemitism in the early 1930s. They wanted to learn the language quickly so they could move to England if they needed to (Bénesty-Sroka, 1996).

When Auntie Léa arrived in Germany, the country was already in the middle of an economic crisis. The Depression in Germany had begun in 1927 or 1928, a year and a bit before the crisis hit the United States in 1929. By the middle of 1931, production and employment had been declining for more than three years. The economic crisis quickly turned into a political crisis. Political parties in Germany, both Left and Right, were unable to form stable governments. Auntie Léa joined other university students in demonstrations organized by the unions and the Left, and then she joined the Communist Party.[16] When Sophie Bissonnette asked Auntie Léa why, she told her it was because people in the Communist Party were prepared to take action to improve economic conditions, not just talk about them. The Roback family's commitment to do something about injustices once again shaped Auntie Léa's response to the hardship and despair she was witnessing.

> Well, I wanted to do something. I don't know . . . It bothers me when things seem unfair. And when we would discuss things at university . . . There was already a group of them there, from different faculties. And so . . . when I arrived at university, I immediately joined the Communist Party, because that's where the action was. The other groups held a lot of meetings, [like] the Sozialdemokraten [Social Democrats] and Sozialisten [Socialists]. It was all very intellectual, and I had had it up to here with all that. So, I joined the communists (Joining the Communist Party in Berlin (1932), 2023).

Auntie Léa reported something similar to Nicole Lacelle.

> It wasn't so much the philosophy (that attracted me) as much as the conviction that one must act, try to reach a goal, that's what interested me (Lacelle and Roback, 2005, p. 62).

Becoming a member of the communist student group in Berlin wasn't easy. Writing about Auntie Léa's experience joining the group, Merrily Weisbord described her reception as "chilly" (Weisbord, 2022, p. 44).

> She had gone to the working-class district in the old part of Berlin and had waited outside the meeting room while a fellow student reported what he had learned from her: no, she had not been in the movement in Canada; yes, she had marched with workers in Paris and in anti-fascist rallies in Berlin … [Inside the meeting room] they looked at her as though she was a street-walker [because of the clothes she was wearing]. Who was she? What was she? She could speak English, French, German, Yiddish. They could tell by her face that she was a Jew … (Weisbord, 2022, p. 45).

Auntie Léa had written out her request to join the student group before the meeting. At the interview, she was asked to repeat her request. Weisbord writes that Auntie Léa told the meeting leaders she wanted to fight the rise of the Nazi Party, which had become the leading party of the Right. She also told them she had gotten her "wits sharpened" at the 1929 May Day demonstration in Berlin when she and her friends had been attacked on campus by law students (Weisbord, 2022, p. 45). She watched how the police protected the law students who were responsible for initiating the violence and she watched as they bashed in the heads and broke the noses of her friends.

After Auntie Léa was accepted into the communist student group she began her training by handing out leaflets, selling the communist newspaper, and organizing a benefit art exhibit called "Women In Need." The exhibit featured drawings by Käthe Kollwitz[17], whose work expressed the anguish of the victims of poverty and war (Weisbord, 2022, p. 45). As Weisbord writes, Auntie Léa's work for the Communist Party was the beginning of a way of life, a way for her to act and "do something" in the face of inhumanity (Weisbord, 2022, p. 46).

The rise of Hitler

With the absence of solidarity between the politically left parties in Germany, the National Socialist German Workers' Party gained political power. The members of the party were called Nazis, and as discussed in Chapter 2, the party was radically right-wing, fascist, antisemitic, anticommunist, and antidemocratic (United States Holocaust Memorial Museum, 2022a).

When the Nazi movement first began in the early 1920s, it was small, ineffective, and marginal. In 1928, the Nazi Party won less than three percent of the national vote in elections to the German parliament. However, beginning in 1930, the Nazi Party started to win more votes, largely because of the economic and political crisis in Germany. The German government was unable to address the problems of unemployment, hunger, poverty, and homelessness. Germany was politically divided, which made the passing of new laws almost impossible because of disagreements in the German parliament. Many Germans lost faith in their leaders' ability to govern. Radical political groups like the Nazi Party took advantage of the economic and political chaos and worked to gain the support of Germans who were fed up with the political stalemate. The Nazi Party promised to fix the economy and put people back to work; return Germany to the status of a great European, and even world, power; regain territory Germany had lost in World War I; create a strong, authoritarian German government; and unite all Germans along racial and ethnic lines. The Nazis also, as discussed in Chapter 2, played on people's hopes, fears, and prejudices by blaming both the Jews and Communists for the country's economic and social problems (United States Holocaust Memorial Museum, 2022a).

While Hitler and the Nazi Party were not directly elected to power, their success in the two 1932 elections made it difficult for the German government to govern the country without their political support. Hitler and the Nazis refused to work with the other political parties that had been elected. When Hitler demanded to be appointed as Chancellor of Germany, President Paul von Hindenburg initially resisted the demand. However, in early 1933 he gave in. Hitler was appointed Chancellor of Germany on 30 January 1933 (United States Holocaust Memorial Museum, 2022a).

By the end of 1932, some of Auntie Léa's professors and comrades in the Communist Party told her she needed to leave Germany as soon as possible to escape the growing violence of both anti-communism and antisemitism. She left reluctantly, and upon her return to Canada, joined the Communist Party in Montreal, where she could put what she had learned about political organizing in Berlin to use.

With the appointment of Adolf Hitler as Chancellor, life in Germany not only became more dangerous for the Jews, it also became dangerous for gay men and lesbian women. One month after he was sworn in as Chancellor, Hitler banned gay and lesbian bars and journals. All the gains German women had made under the Weimar Republic (which governed between 9 November 1918 and 23 March 1933) were reversed. Several months later, on 6 May 1933, the Nazis destroyed Dr. Magnus Hirschfeld's Institute for Sexual Research, which at the time was internationally well-known for its extensive library, its groundbreaking research on sexuality and homosexuality, and its calls for sexual reform to protect gays and lesbians from arrest and prison (Setterington, 2013, p. 25).

Several days later, on 10 May, the Nazis held large book burnings and burned the thousands of books held by the Institute. In June 1935, the Nazis passed a law that punished any act that could be construed as homosexual. Even an embrace was criminally punishable. Then, two years later, on 15 September 1935, the Nuremberg Laws – the Laws for the Protection of German Blood and German Honor – were passed. This was the law that deprived German Jews of citizenship and rights. In 1936, the Sachsenhausen concentration camp opened near Berlin. Men caught in homosexual acts were sent there and to other similar camps (which were not yet death camps). Romani and Sinti people (a community within the Romani community), as well as Jehovah's Witnesses, were also arrested and sent to concentration camps (Setterington, 2013, pp. 163–166).

Uncle Harry and Auntie Betty did not leave Berlin with Auntie Léa in early 1933. They stayed on so Uncle Harry could finish his medical degree. But in May 1933, Uncle Harry was arrested with some friends because they refused to respond to a "Heil Hitler" from two Nazis in the street. Auntie Léa recalls that Betty managed to get Harry out of prison, and two days later, he was in England. Auntie Léa also remembers that Auntie Betty stayed behind with their baby daughter Maud (Lacelle and Roback, 2005, p. 128).

The story of how Harry, Betty, and Maud escaped from Germany is remembered differently by their son Howard Roback who was born after the family returned to North America. In a 2022 email correspondence between Howard and my cousin Melanie Leavitt, Howard reported that his father sent Betty and Maud back to Montreal *before* he himself left Berlin (Melanie Leavitt, personal communication, 25 March 2025). In his email to Melanie, Howard also mentioned that he had been contacted by a historian at Harvard University who was writing an article about a doctor who, along with two other Jewish medical students in Berlin, was "pulled out by the Gestapo for particularly cruel treatment." The historian told Howard that Harry Roback was one of the other two medical students and that he was looking for information about "why the three had been taken to Gestapo headquarters and beaten badly." As mentioned earlier, the answer to this question in Auntie Léa's recollection was because they had refused to respond to a "Heil Hitler" from two Nazis on the street.

When Auntie Léa is asked by Nicole Lacelle what year Harry left Berlin, she says she isn't sure, but she knows he was gone before *Kristallnacht*, the Night of Broken Glass, in 1938. *Kristallnacht*, which means "The Night of Broken Glass" in English, was a night of violence that targeted Jews. Jewish-owned businesses, synagogues, and homes were vandalized and destroyed. Jewish men were rounded up and taken to concentration camps, making it the first time Nazi leaders made massive arrests of Jews just because they were Jews, without any other cause for arrest (United States Holocaust Memorial Museum, 2019).[18] A year later, in 1939, Hitler initiated a decree that empowered physicians to grant a "mercy" death to the mentally and physically challenged, or any person considered to be genetically defective. The same year, the Nazis began to deport German Jews to Poland, and by 1942, they began mass gassing of Jews in the concentration camps in Poland, which had become death camps. By the end of the war in May 1945, six million Jews had been murdered by the Nazis (Setterington, 2013, pp. 167–169).

Although her years in Berlin were some of the most exciting and enriching years of her life, Auntie Léa never returned to Berlin. When interviewer Ghila Bénesty-Sroka asked her if she had ever gone back, Auntie Léa answered, "No, the people I knew there are dead. I sent packages, but I never knew if they received them."

Joining the Communist Party in Montreal

After leaving Berlin, Auntie Léa returned to Montreal and went to live with her mother and father in their home in the neighbourhood of Outremont. Uncle Harry, Auntie Betty, and Maud moved to Cleveland, Ohio, in the United States where Harry could find work as a psychiatrist.

Beginning life again in Montreal, Auntie Léa joined the Montreal branch of the Communist Party of Canada (CPC). Being a member of the CPC at the time was risky as the party had been declared an illegal organization in 1931 under Section 98 of the Canadian *Criminal Code*. Section 98 made it illegal to "sell, speak, write or publish" anything related to an "unlawful association" (Lévesque and Clapperton-Richard, 2018). While the definition of "unlawful association" was vague, it was meant to include groups that advocated the use of force to bring about political change. This included many left and labour organizations. While the Canadian government repealed the provision in 1936, being a member of the CPC before then meant risking spending time in prison.

Section 98 was created by the federal government in 1919 to limit the power and influence of labour and left activists after the Winnipeg General Strike. The Winnipeg General Strike of 1919 was one of the largest strikes in Canadian history. For four weeks between 15 May and 25 June 1919, more than 30,000 workers left their jobs to fight for improved working conditions. Factories, shops, transit, and city services were all shut down. The strike resulted in arrests, injuries, and the deaths of two protestors, but did not immediately succeed in empowering workers and improving job conditions. However, the strike did help unite working-class people in Canada, who continued to advocate for better working conditions. As well some of the strikers from the Winnipeg General Strike worked to establish a left-of-centre federal political party, which today is known as the New Democratic Party (NDP) (Reilly, 2006). Founded in 1961, the NDP has formed the government in several provinces but never nationally. Today, the federal NDP is committed to issues of affordability, climate action, improved health care, and Reconciliation with Canada's Indigenous Peoples (NDP, 2019).

Needing to financially contribute to her parents' household, Auntie Léa found a job working for the Young Women's Hebrew Association (YWHA). The YWHA played an important role in the Jewish community in Montreal. At the time all social and recreational services in Quebec were segregated along religious and linguistic lines. During the Depression, there was no work for young people and "a lack of everything," even food (Lacelle and Roback, 2005, p. 131). The YWHA was established in a big house on St. Urbain Street, which was located in the heart of the Jewish immigrant, working-class neighbourhood of Montreal. There were always young people hanging around the house, so the staff brought them inside and gave them something to do. Auntie Léa organized programming for the children: dramatic presentations, art classes, and outings to galleries. She also "cajoled and blackmailed" the women of the board of the YWHA into giving her money to buy essentials for the young people she worked with. She also organized an unofficial Marxist study group (Weisbord, 2022, p. 47). Sunday mornings the staff would show movies to the children and youth, and serve snacks, like ice cream cones. Those who could pay an admission fee, did; those who couldn't, didn't. Every Sunday about 100 young people would show up for the movies (Lacelle and Roback, 2005, p. 131).

In 1934, Auntie Léa left her YWHA job to follow a lover who was in the Soviet Union and spent three months there. He wanted to marry her, but Auntie Léa decided it was not her place to stay in the Soviet Union. She needed to go back to Montreal and try to create change in Quebec. She explained:

> I told myself, first of all, I don't have the right to come here and sit at their table, because it was hard, very hard: the war of 1914–18, the [1917] Revolution, getting things back in order, they had their hands full. No, I'm a member of a party, the Communist Party, and I have to go back home and try to do something (Lacelle and Roback, 2005, p. 133).

After returning from the Soviet Union, Auntie Léa found a job at Cedar Knolls School, a school for young offenders near Gloversville in the state of New York. She didn't stay there very long. She was incensed by a comment made by one of the women on the board of directors who had no idea what the lives of the girls Auntie Léa worked with were like. The school was on a hill and had a view of the Rockefeller estate.

> One day, a Mrs. Bache, whose husband was a big shot on the Wall Street Stock Exchange, came and said, "Isn't it wonderful for those girls to be able to see the Rockefeller estate!" So, I replied, "What a great chance this is, hey, through bars!" (Lacelle and Roback, 2005, p. 135).

When an opportunity to leave her job at the school came up, Auntie Léa took it.

Auntie Léa meets Fred Rose

While Auntie Léa was working at the Cedar Knolls School she came back to Montreal for a weekend visit. During the visit, she was told that Fred Rose, a Communist Party member was going to run in the upcoming provincial election. Like her parents Fanny and Moishe, Fred Rose was a Jewish immigrant from Poland. He arrived in Canada at the age of ten and trained to become an electrician and union organizer (Anctil and Woodsworth, 2021, p. 241).

The year before Rose had run in the federal election as a candidate in the Montreal riding of Cartier. After losing, he decided to run in the 1936 Quebec provincial election and asked Auntie Léa to be his campaign manager. Once again Auntie Léa's ability to cross borders between French, English and Yiddish was extremely valuable. As Melanie Leavitt explains:

> She's somebody who is perfectly at ease in Yiddish, in English and in French. She's somebody who's well-versed in all of the political terminology, and she has the consciousness of somebody, you know, of a good Communist Party member. But also, she's somebody who's fearless, who's not afraid to stand on the street corner, hand out pamphlets, go door-to-door and canvass (Jewish Public Library, 2024c, *recollections,* Episode 3).

When Fred Rose asked Auntie Léa to manage his campaign, she told him she had never done anything like that in her life. He told her she would learn along the way, but he didn't have much money to pay her. For Auntie Léa, money wasn't an issue. She could live with her parents and eat her meals at home. Despite not having the right to vote in Quebec because she was a woman (women didn't get the right to vote in Quebec until 1940), Auntie Léa decided to leave her job at the school and learn how to run Rose's campaign (Lacelle and Roback, 2005, pp. 135–136).

Fred Rose and Auntie Léa raised money for the campaign from Jewish refugees living in Rose's riding who had immigrated from Eastern Europe and Hitler's Germany. They knew what fascism meant and wanted to stop it. They also received donations from immigrants living in the riding who had lived in Finland, Hungary, Italy, the Czech Republic, and Poland. They too had seen fascism first-hand. Their donations were delivered to the campaign office wrapped up in packages of local ethnic newspapers. Inside were lots of pennies and sometimes some nickels. Once or twice, Auntie Léa found a dollar bill. The donors also went campaigning door-to-door telling people, "We have to see that Comrade Rose gets in!" (Weisbord, 2022, p. 87). Fred Rose lost the 1936 Quebec provincial election but several years later he ran again in a 1943 federal by-election and won. Rose became the first Canadian Communist Member of Parliament (MP) to be elected, and as of today, remains the only Communist MP to be elected to parliament.

The Modern Book Shop and the Padlock Law

Around the same time as Auntie Léa began working on Fred Rose's campaign, she also helped open and manage the Modern Book Shop, one of Montreal's first and most influential Marxist bookstores. In the 1930s, there were two leftist bookstores in Montreal, and both were closely linked to the Communist Party. The first was the Hidden Book Shop on Saint Catherine Street. It was managed by a brother and sister team, Ann and Sam (Sol) Feigelman between 1933 and 1934. The Feigelmans could not sell Communist books and newspapers freely because of Section 98 of the *Criminal Code*. In fact, in June 1933, the Hidden Book Shop was raided, and the Feigelmans were charged and found guilty of selling seditious literature that encouraged people to revolt against the state (Lévesque and Clapperton-Richard, 2018). The second leftist bookstore was the Modern Book Shop that Auntie Léa set up. It sold books listed in the Index as well as progressive novels, journals, pamphlets, and newspapers, such as *The Daily Clarion* from Toronto, and *Clarté*, a Montreal weekly paper that began publishing in 1935.[19]

While the Canadian law concerning seditious literature had changed by 1936, it was still a politically repressive time to be selling Marxist material in Quebec (Lévesque and Clapperton-Richard, 2018). Section 98 had been repealed, but the newly elected Union Nationale government in Quebec, headed by Premier Maurice Duplessis, together with the Catholic Church launched a vast anti-communist campaign in October 1936. The campaign was part of the Red Scare and hysteria that emerged (particularly in the United States) following the 1917 Revolution in the Soviet Union. Communists were perceived as a threat to the government and the Church, a threat that would intensify during the Cold War after World War Two. Bookshops were among the first places to be targeted in crackdowns on published communist material. Auntie Léa found herself confronting the police, who were monitoring the selling of "subversive" books and newspapers. She also had to deal with threatening letters, vandalism, and broken windows. For example, in a digital research project called *The Radical History Poster Project*, Montreal history professor Andrée Lévesque has posted the contents of a letter the bookshop received in 1936. The letter said:

> Last Warning. We give you three days to close everything or else we put dynamite around the Modern Book Shop. The police are with us and you know it. We will be there

this week. We are and will remain Fascists (Lévesque and Clapperton-Richard, 2018).

A few months later, in March 1937, the Quebec legislature unanimously passed The Act to Protect the Province Against Communistic Propaganda," commonly known as the Padlock Law, which allowed the police to close down and padlock the door of any premises used to disseminate "Bolshevik" propaganda. The Bolsheviks, led by Vladimir Lenin, were a far-left faction of the Marxist Russian Social Democratic Labour Party founded in 1898 in Minsk. The party later became the Communist Party of the Soviet Union.

The Padlock Law made it unlawful to print, to publish, or to distribute any writing that propagated or tended to propagate Communism or Bolshevism, and it applied to bookshops, meeting halls, even private houses, making it increasingly difficult to organize meetings and buy and sell leftist literature. In her interviews with Merrily Weisbord, Auntie Léa mentions travelling to New York City to smuggle in books that were banned by the Index (Weisbord, 2022, p. 47).

Andrée Lévesque writes that at the time, left bookshops such as the Modern Book Shop were more than just places where books and magazines were sold. Meetings were held there, new publications were launched there – providing a community space for leftists to connect with other leftists. It was at the Modern Book Shop where Auntie Léa Roback met communist doctor Norman Bethune. Today Bethune is well-known for his work to develop mobile medical units and surgical instruments which saved many lives in the Spanish Civil War where he performed blood transfusions in the midst of heavy fighting. In Sophie Bissonnette's film, Auntie Léa talks about the impact the Padlock Law had on the Modern Book Shop and her family:

> … the cops came [to the bookstore]. Not the uniformed cops. The Red Squad. We recognized them right off … They came when we [the family] lived in the north end, near Outremont. They'd often come to take my books. One cover was red. "Ah ha! That's Communist." It wasn't Communist.
>
> Mama never scolded me. Neither Mom nor Dad were Communist. They supported me though. After all, we were at home … These guys came up. Four, five, or six of them were riffling through books. Mama was indignant. And she didn't hide it (*Des lumières dans la grande noirceur*, 1991).

Commenting on the impact of the Padlock Law on the members of the Communist Party, Merrily Weisbord writes that rather than frightening the communists into submission, the law made them angry and determined. Auntie Léa told Weisbord that the home where she lived with her parents was visited five times (Weisbord, 2022, p. 91).

> We had them coming up to the house in droves. The whole of Querbes Avenue had to know the police were coming to the Robacks (Weisbord, 2022, p. 91).

The police took Auntie Léa's leather souvenir case from Grenoble, her address book with notes from friends in Europe, her library of works by Marx – which, because the books were in German, she knew the police couldn't read. While police visits to their homes didn't stop Auntie Léa and her comrades from doing the political work they had undertaken, it did make their work more difficult. It was her anger, Auntie Léa told Weisbord, that kept her going.

> With such things we don't get stronger; they frighten the children [living in homes with communist parents]; but it showed how they feared us, and through my anger I was able to continue working. They had no right to do that when they spoke of democracy (Weisbord, 2022, p. 91).

So, despite the threatening letters, vandalism, and visits from the Red Squad, Auntie Léa continued to manage the Modern Book Shop until 1936 when she was offered a new job: the position of Educational Director with the International Ladies' Garment Workers Union (ILGWU), which was working to unionize dressmaking workers in Montreal. While Auntie Léa knew the bookstore was a valued space where the communist community could meet, she also knew that unionizing the workers in the dressmaking industry was important. She accepted the ILGWU position and was given the task of developing an education program that would support the unionization of the dressmaking industry in Montreal. Auntie Léa's work with the ILGWU is discussed in Chapter 4.

Leaving the Communist Party

As the Cold War between the East and the West deepened, Canadian Jews began to receive reports that the Communist Party in the Soviet Union was repressing Yiddish culture and the people who were trying to keep it alive. When the Red Army took over Berlin at the end of the Second World War in May 1945, the "great historic centres of Ashkenazic [European Jewish] culture" in Poland, Lithuania, Hungary, Romania, and Czechoslovakia became subject to the influence and power of the Soviet Union (Anctil and Woodsworth, 2021, p. 240). The reports of the repression of Yiddish culture, which was so important to Eastern European Jewish people living in Montreal and other parts of Canada, were alarming. Then in 1956, at the 20th Congress of the Communist Party of the Soviet Union, Soviet Premier Nikita Khrushchev released a report that detailed the execution of some of the Soviet Union's most well-known and respected Yiddish poets on 12 August 1952 – a night that became known as the Night of the Murdered Poets, or in Yiddish, *Harugey malkut funem Ratnfarband*. The release of The Khrushchev Report, or the Khrushchev revelations, was the first time Canadian communists (including Auntie Léa) say they discovered the atrocities committed by Stalin in the Soviet Union. The report sparked outrage in the Canadian Jewish diaspora, including Jewish Montreal. As Pierre Anctil writes, the last surviving enclave of Jewish creativity in Eastern Europe had now been destroyed (Anctil and Woodsworth, 2021, p. 246).

As discussed in Chapter 2, Auntie Léa grew up listening to the Yiddish stories her father brought into their home. These stories both expressed the many injustices in the world and contained dreams of a *shenere un besere velt*—a better and more beautiful world. The dreams of a better world fuelled Auntie Léa and other Jewish activists in confronting oppression through their work with the Communist Party. The execution of Yiddish poets in the Soviet Union shattered many people's faith that communism in the Soviet Union could create a better and more beautiful world. While many Jews left the Communist Party of Canada after Khrushchev's report was released, Auntie Léa didn't leave the Party until 1958, two years after the Khrushchev Report was released. Her reasons for doing so are discussed below. However, several years prior to the release of the report, Auntie Léa's focus and energy began to shift as she added new family commitments to her political commitments. In 1952, Auntie Léa's brother Michael was diagnosed with cancer. Michael had two daughters: Judith, who was eight or nine years old at the time, and Barbara, who was only two. Auntie Léa's mother Fanny wanted her to take care of Barbara. "So," Auntie Léa told Nicole Lacelle, "I took care of the youngest" (Lacelle and Roback, 2005, pp. 171–172). My cousin Barbara remembers sleeping over at Fanny and Auntie Léa's house and Auntie Léa talking about how Barbara always woke up early – at 6:00 a.m.

After both their father Michael and their mother Gertrude died, Gertrude's sister Ida came to live with Judith and Barbara. Their Roback aunts and uncles helped out financially and kept up a close relationship with their nieces. Judith and Barbara also received support from their parents' Communist Party friends and acquaintances. Both Michael and Gertrude had been part of the Jewish leftist social circle in Montreal, and Judith and Barbara were friendly with children from other leftist families such as writer Merrily Weisbord whose historical research on the Communist Party in Canada appears in this chapter. Judith remembers:

> The summer camp we went to (a hikeable distance from Weisbord Acres, where writer Merrily Weisbord and her family had a collection of cottages for themselves and to

rent or be bought by "likeminded people") was begun by the Party, and then was run by UJPO [the United Jewish People's Order], a secular progressive Jewish organization (Judith Roback, personal communication, 20 November 2024).

In a 2024 email exchange Judith told me, "We were surrounded by the warmth felt for our parents."

Almost all of Judith's social activities were with the children of her parents' friends, and her first cousins Kathy and Francie, who were Leo's daughters (Leo was Auntie Léa's youngest brother; Michael, Judith, and Barbara's father was her second youngest brother). Right up into high school and university, Judith remembers her social life being centred around people she knew from camp or children of the like-minded people her parents had known. On weekends, she hung out with her leftist family friends, listened to folk music and protest songs, and went to "serious" cinema. Even Judith's optician was a part of her leftist social circle. When she was a student at McGill University and needed new glasses, the optician didn't ask Judith to pay for them. When Judith insisted on paying, the optician made up a reduced price (Judith Roback, personal communication, 24 November 2024).

The financial and emotional support Judith and Barbara received from their family and family friends allowed both of them to attend university and pursue professional careers. Judith earned a PhD in Anthropology, taught in universities, and later worked in the Toronto Public Library. Today she is retired from the library, lives in Toronto with her partner Richard, and volunteers in the

Library and Archives department at the Art Gallery of Ontario. Barbara became a psychologist and then a medical doctor. She raised twin sons, Joshua and Noah, with her partner Marc, and now lives in Victoria, British Columbia.

In a recent conversation Judith and I had about the revelations made by Khrushchev in 1952, Judith reflected, "it is difficult to imagine the depth of disillusionment, sadness, pain, and anger of all those who had been so committed to their Communist ideals for so many years" (Judith Roback, personal communication, 20 November 2024). Yet, Judith noted, many or most of her parents' friends and acquaintances retained their communist ideals and values and found ways to put them into action.

Auntie Léa left the Communist Party in 1958 two years after the Khrushchev report was released. Between 1952, the year her brother Michael was diagnosed with cancer, and 1958, the year he died, Auntie Léa continued attending meetings and volunteering for the Party. When she left in 1958, it was for two reasons. She wanted to be available to support Michael and his family during the last stages of his illness, and she no longer had confidence that the leadership of the Canadian Communist Party understood the political needs of Quebec. She told Nicole Lacelle, "I resigned in '58 because of the national question..." and then she added, "at the same time, my brother Michael became seriously ill" (Lacelle and Roback, 2005, p. 180).

The national question Auntie Léa referred to is the ongoing political and cultural debate around the status, identity, and future of the province of Quebec within Canada. The debate centres on whether Quebec should remain a province within Canada, seek greater autonomy, or pursue independence as a sovereign nation. The historical roots of the national question lie in Quebec's history as a predominantly French-speaking society within an English-speaking majority country. Quebec's sovereignty movement, led by the political party the Parti Québécois, has argued for Quebec to become an independent country to preserve its distinct language and culture. In 1980 and 1995, referendums were held on the issue of sovereignty. In both referendums the "No" side, which voted against sovereignty won. However, it is important to note that in the second referendum, it was a narrow win, with only 50.6% of the ballots voting "No" against independence.

The reason the Communist Party priorities were in conflict with the priorities of Quebec nationalism – and the needs and concerns of francophone members from Quebec – had to do with the fact that ideologically, national identity was considered secondary to the more important issue of class identity. However, even after leaving the Communist Party, Auntie Léa always maintained that the years she had spent working for the party had been important and had shaped her in a variety of ways. "I owe a lot to the Communist Party," she told Lacelle, "because I had the chance to grow and learn" (Lacelle and Roback, 2005, p. 136). As a member of the Communist Party, Auntie Léa was given the opportunity to open the Modern Book Shop, run Fred Rose's campaign, and design union education programming for members of the International Ladies' Garment Workers Union (ILGWU). Auntie Léa's exciting and successful work with the ILGWU and RCA Victor is discussed next.

4
Montreal

Fighting for workers' rights (1936–1952)

> The fact that I was not alone, that I had to speak on behalf of all those who did not dare, gave me courage. They respected the employer solely because he was the boss. I told them, "The boss needs us. If he didn't have us, he would be forced to take the iron or the broom himself. He is not God." They were afraid of losing their jobs. I tried to make them understand that if we supported each other, no one would lose anything.
>
> – Léa Roback[20]

***

In 1936, Auntie Léa started working as the educational director for the International Ladies' Garment Workers' Union (ILGWU). The so-called "International" unions were based in the United States, and organized unions in other countries such as Mexico and Canada from their office in New York. At the time, workers in the Montreal dressmaking industry worked up to 80 hours a week for low wages and had to deal with the deafening noise of a variety of machines and unwanted sexual advances. Unionizing the dressmaking industry was difficult. Historian Melanie Leavitt explains:

> … despite the fact that Montreal was the capital of clothing production in all of Canada, the unions were having a tremendous amount of difficulty in successfully reaching the workers and getting their foot in the door into that industry because they were faced with the problems of, well, for one, a political and a religious and a social climate that was quite hostile towards unionization, but also because they were faced with a workforce, particularly in the dress industry, that was primarily female, about 80% female, but also predominantly French Canadian Catholic.
>
> And that was the workforce that the left-wing international unions – that were mostly run and organized by Eastern European Jewish left-wingers – were not really able to [reach] … they had been making small inroads into the industry, but it was mostly limited to the Jewish workforce (Jewish Public Library, 2024c, *recollections*, Episode 3).

For years, Leavitt says, it was considered impossible to unionize French-Canadian women. Organizers believed they "were not organizable" and pointed to the influence of the Catholic Church as one of the reasons why. In an article about unionizing the dressmaking industry in the 1930s, Sophia Cutler writes that at the time, the Catholic Church dominated all aspects of francophone life. Sunday sermons demonized the Jewish-led unions and urged parishioners to join their own compliant Catholic unions or make use of the charities run by the Church to supplement their wages (Cutler, 2017, p. 9). Another reason it was difficult for the International Ladies' Garment Workers' Union to unionize workers was that it was an American union with limited understanding of what it meant to organize workers in Quebec. Having grown up in Quebec, Auntie Léa had that understanding.

In 1936, Rose Pesotta, the vice-president of the International Ladies' Garment Workers' Union, was sent to Montreal to the organize French-Canadian women workers. Rose Pesotta was a Jewish immigrant from Ukraine who had started her working life in New York City as a seamstress in the dressmaking industry. She began full-time organizing for the ILGWU in 1933. Auntie Léa described her as a "wonderful organizer," who didn't go by her Jewish family name. She called herself Pesotta and told people she was Spanish because at that time, "Jews [were] not so kosher [acceptable]" (Harris and Roback, 1988).

Before arriving in Montreal Rose Pesotta worked in Los Angeles, California, organizing Mexican women dressmakers. In her biography of Pesotta, Elizabeth Leeder writes that like the French-Canadian women dressmakers, the Mexican women dressmakers were also thought to be "unorganizable" because of cultural and family pressures for them not to work outside the home and the assumption that they would work for very little money (Leeder, 1993, p. 57). In her campaign to organize the workers, Pesotta bought spots on Spanish-speaking radio stations, published a newspaper in Spanish and English, and visited workers in their homes and community shops (Leeder, 1993, p. 57). Pesotta also set up an education program for the workers in Los Angeles. Having had the opportunity to attend summer courses at Labor College in New York State, Pesotta believed that union education was a means of empowering workers in many aspects of their lives, not just their working lives. She established courses in economics, social and political issues, public speaking and writing. The courses were held in the ILGWU union hall, and Pesotta both taught classes herself and hired other teachers (Leeder, 1993, p. 62).

Auntie Léa and Rose Pesotta

When Rose Pesotta arrived in Montreal several years later, she wanted to replicate her Los Angeles educational programming and started to look for an Educational Director. As Pesotta herself did not speak French, and had never lived in Quebec, she needed to hire a reliable person who could relate to the French-Canadian workers. Auntie Léa, who grew up in Quebec and could speak Yiddish and English as well as French, was an excellent match for the position. As Leavitt tells us:

> These were women that [Auntie Léa] could relate to. These were women that were just the same as her friends during her childhood or the neighbors that she grew up around (Jewish Public Library, 2024c, *recollections,* Episode 3).

Rose Pesotta's first task in Montreal was to organize bilingual (French and English) radio broadcasts to recruit members for the ILGWU. The broadcasts talked about the low wages Montreal dressmakers were getting in comparison to the dressmakers in Toronto and the United States. The broadcasts also reported that the International Ladies' Garment Workers' Union had already won a living wage and improved working conditions for more than 200,000 needle workers across North America (Pesotta,

1944, p. 264). Immediately, Pesotta came into conflict with the Catholic Church which had helped factory owners organize their own company unions (Leeder, 1993, p. 73). Labelled as an "outside agitator," Pesotta quickly discovered the power the church wielded in Quebec. In her autobiography *Bread upon the Waters* Pesotta wrote:

> ... the Catholic Church dominated all phases of life in Quebec, political, economic, social, moral, cultural. Many of the clergy, in impassioned Sunday sermons, warned their parishioners against our union, and openly advocated that Jews, radicals of all shades and "disruptive foreigners" (meaning labour organizers from the United States) be driven out of the province (Pesotta, 1944, p. 270).

While Pesotta herself was an anarchist and atheist, and was opposed to organized religion, she understood the respect workers felt for the church. She did not argue against the church but used the teachings of the church to recruit union members by drawing on the work of Catholic priests in the United States who supported unionization and striking for better wages and working conditions (Leeder, 1993, p. 73).

Pesotta's unionization efforts were unexpectedly supported by many Jewish factory owners who didn't want a Catholic union operating in their shops. As Auntie Léa explains, many of the Jewish factory owners had been cutters, tailors, the "aristocrats" of the industry, who had married the daughter of a man who owned his factory.

> The owners were Jews and wanted to do business with Jews ... some Jewish bosses [said], "We don't want to

have a Catholic union, we're Jews, we don't want the priest to come and tell us what to do …" (Lacelle and Roback, 2005, pp. 139–140).

In addition to the influence of the Catholic Church, traditional thinking and practices around gender roles within the ILGWU itself were also an obstacle to organizing the women dressmakers. As Leavitt explained earlier, before Pesotta arrived the local ILGWU leadership in Montreal was dominated by skilled male workers who were often English-speaking and Jewish. Pesotta herself was the only woman on the executive board of the ILGWU in the United States, whose membership was composed of 85% women. A few years later, she would be pushed out of her leadership role in the ILGWU.

Sophia Cutler writes that while the "unskilled" women union members were expected to participate in workers' strikes, they were often excluded from decision-making. The leaders saw themselves as "father figures" for women workers in the dressmaking industry and didn't treat them as peers or comrades. This made many women sceptical about joining the union (Cutler, 2017, p. 10). As historian Mercedes Steedman, cited by Cutler, points out:

> [T]he union offices were places for men to gather, play cards, and talk politics. Only at strike time did the union halls open up their doors to women workers and provide gathering places and social activities that women were able to plan and participate in (Cutler, 2017, p. 10).

As well, men typically worked as cutters and pressers in the industry. They held "skilled" jobs that made them, as Auntie Léa says above, aristocrats of the industry. Women were employed as "unskilled" sewing-machine operators. Men operated the heavy machines which required skill and dexterity to manoeuvre – skills the women were thought not to have or need to operate the sewing machines. In reality, however, the categories of "skilled" and "unskilled" workers were meaningless. They had no relation to the actual strength, dexterity, or skill capacity individual workers possessed. Cutler writes that at least one factory inspector at the time conceded that although women's work was "generally regarded as light," in reality it was "hard and most exacting. Women engaged in it are liable to have to work overtime more frequently than in other trades" (Cutler, 2017, p. 10). The distinction between skilled and unskilled labour was used to justify lower wages for women's "unskilled" labour. Women were paid on average half of what the men were paid (Leavitt, personal communication, 25 March 2025).

Creating unity and solidarity

Auntie Léa's work to establish language classes, courses, and social activities in the union hall created a more welcoming space for women workers. In her role as Educational Director of the ILGWU, with the support of a team of Francophone organizers, Auntie Léa educated the women dressmakers in union activism, and offered them French and English language classes. There were also courses on journalism, music, public speaking, and the history of the Canadian labour movement, which were held in the ILGWU union hall. In a 1986 interview with Quebec sociologist and activist Nicole Lacelle (republished in 2005), Auntie Léa said this about her work:

> We worked on setting up a library and teaching French or English to those who did not speak it. We also tackled the issue of piecework. Damn it, we had to put that in the trash. Sewing buttons or putting on a zipper, making buttonholes, all of that bang, bang, bang, it was done by the piece. How much did it pay? Two and a half cents to sew a button, to hem; imagine how many hems you had to do [to make a living !] (Lacelle and Roback, 2005, pp. 141–142).

Another important issue connected to the issue of piecework was the issue of favouritism and unwanted sexual advances. As Auntie Léa explains

> … back in the day, there was a lot of favoritism; some workers wanted a good batch of pieces to sew [at home], well… the foreman or the small boss "took advantage of them" as they would say (Lacelle and Roback, 2005, pp. 140–141).

The women workers wanted to fight for the right to their bodies – the right not to be harassed by the designers, the boss, or the foreman (*Des lumières dans la grande noirceur,* 1991).

Alongside classes and discussions about workers' rights, Auntie Léa and Rose Pesotta organized social activities such as a choir, orchestra, theatre, sports, parties, and cultural festivals which provided opportunities for the English-speaking Jewish workers and French-speaking Catholic workers to meet each other. Besides these two groups of workers, there were also Russian, Italian, Portuguese, Chinese, and Black women working in the factories. Auntie Léa also published a newsletter called "The Organizer/*L'Organistrice*" in both French and English. A copy of the newsletter is available in the Léa Roback archives at the Jewish Public Library. Spending time learning and socializing together promoted the development of unity and solidarity among the women workers, two key values necessary for negotiations between the workers and the factory owners. As Auntie Léa says in the quote that opens this chapter, building unity and solidarity among the workers meant that no one had to negotiate with factory owners alone. Because Auntie Léa knew she was not alone in fighting for better wages and better working conditions, she had the courage she needed to speak on behalf of those who were afraid to speak.

The dressmaker strike of 1937

In January 1937, after a successful recruitment drive that included handing out leaflets at the doors of factories in the early morning as the workers were going in, the dressmakers received their first charter. The first goal for Local 262 of the ILGWU in Montreal was to create a contract with manufacturers that ensured union recognition, and better hours and pay. But the Montreal Dress Manufacturers' Guild – an association of factory owners – refused to recognize the union. On 15 April 1937, just months after getting their charter, Local 262 triggered a surprise general strike against one hundred shops and factories. Rose Pesotta, Auntie Léa and the ILGWU shop stewards led five thousand women workers on the most momentous strike in Canadian dressmaking history.

The strike became known as the Dressmaker Strike of 1937 and the Midinettes Strike. The word "midinettes" is a combination of the French word *midi* (noon) and *dinette* (light lunch) and was used to describe the women who would pour out of the downtown dress factories during their brief lunch break. In her interviews with Sophie Bissonnette and Nicole Lacelle about the strike, Auntie Léa remembers:

> The bosses didn't know that a strike was planned. That night, after the [union] meetings, we spoke with the workers. The next morning, "No pasaran!" "Nobody goes in!" (*Des lumières dans la grande noirceur*, 1991)

> … we went on strike for three weeks, it was great! The women came out, they organized themselves, Jews, French Canadians, immigrants. There were women who never thought they could become shop stewards, yet many did. There was unity! (Lacelle and Roback, 2005, pp. 140–141).

In response to the workers going on strike, the Church, and the government of Quebec led by Premier Maurice Duplessis worked to end it. The highly-ranked clergy in Montreal called for the deportation of Rose Pesotta, who was an American citizen. But on the day she was to be arrested, Pesotta found a place to hide where the police would not find her – under a hair dryer at a beauty salon. She ordered a facial, manicure, and as many other beauty services as she could to avoid the police as long as she could. When the salon closed, she found a secluded restaurant to have dinner in and then went to a movie. She was successful in evading the police. The arrest warrant was never served (Leeder, 1993, p. 74).

In addition to putting out an arrest warrant for Rose Pesotta, the Duplessis government began an anti-communist campaign that targeted and criminalized any form of labour activism. Melanie Leavitt explains that Duplessis used laws such as the Padlock Law to target the labour movement under the guise of fighting the "threat" of Communism. During the Dressmakers' Strike, Duplessis, Catholic Church leaders, and even the leaders of the Catholic unions regularly invoked the accusation that the leaders of the ILGWU were "notorious Communists." The accusation of being Communist was used to undermine the credibility of the ILGWU (and other international unions) and to dissuade French Canadian, Catholic workers from joining their ranks (Leavitt, personal communication, 25 March 2025). Because the International Ladies' Garment Workers' Union was mostly run and organized by Eastern European Jewish left-wingers, the anti-communist campaign was often antisemitic. As Cutler writes, French newspapers such as *La Nation* and *Le Devoir* named ILGWU organizers as "la juiverie internationale" or "the international Jewry" – a label that reflected the long history of antisemitic representations of Jews as a menace that was increasing its numbers and power globally through finance and (contradictorily) communism (Cutler, 2017, p. 11).

But despite the work of the Church and the government to destroy the union, the women workers maintained their solidarity. As one picketer's sign declared, "*Nos races sont multiples, notre but est un*" – "We are many races, but our aim is one" (Cutler, 2017, p. 11). Rose Pesotta and Auntie Léa's work to build alliances across language, culture and religion was successful.

Unified, the women marched on the picket line for 25 days forcing the Montreal Dress Manufacturers' Guild to finally enter into negotiation with the leaders of Local 262. On 10 May, after 14 hours of negotiation, Local 262 won significant improvements to their workers' wages and working conditions. To celebrate, Pesotta decided to attend the ILGWU's annual national convention which was being held in Atlantic City. She brought a large delegation from Montreal with her. The delegation marched up to the platform with a brass band preceding them. They received a standing ovation from the assembly. It was a moment of triumph (Leeder, 1993, p. 74). The 1937 Dressmakers' Strike became the largest strike of women workers in Québec history and would remain so until 1972. As Auntie Léa has said to several interviewers, "Never before had there been a women's strike of such magnitude in Montreal."

Today there is a Parks Canada plaque located at 460 St. Catherine Street West in Montreal that designates the 1937 Dressmakers' Strike as a National Historic Event. It says:

> Led by the International Ladies' Garment Workers Union, this strike was a turning point in the unionization of a key industry in Montréal, then principal centre of clothing production in Canada. In three weeks, Rose Pesotta, Lea Roback, and Yvette Charpentier, among others, rallied a primarily female French-Canadian workforce of more than 5,000 that was regarded by trade unionists as difficult to organize. An example of the essential contributions of Jewish activists within the clothing industry, this successful strike reflected the ability of Jewish and French-Canadian workers to cooperate in a union setting (Parks Canada Directory of Federal Heritage Designations, 2024).

Honoured by Parks Canada for its importance in the evolution of the working relationships between management and labour in the clothing industry" (Parks Canada Directory of Federal Heritage Designations, 2024), Leavitt calls the success of the 1937 Dressmakers' Strike a "monumental moment" that not only paved the way forward for the dressmaking industry but paved the way for important gains in the labour movement across a variety of different sectors. It also paved the way for many important gains for women's rights (Jewish Public Library, 2024c, *recollections,* Episode 3). Auntie Léa's life and work in the women's rights movement is discussed in the next chapter.

Fighting racism in the dressmaking industry

Shortly after the strike ended, Auntie Léa encountered an incident of Black racism in one of the factories that had been unionized. She was working in the union office when a Jewish factory owner telephoned and asked her to send him a draper. Working from the local's seniority list, Auntie Léa picked the draper at the top of the list. She was a Black woman named Hélène, who was a talented draper. Auntie Léa told the owner that she'd arrive in fifteen minutes. Hélène arrived back at the union office half an hour later and told Auntie Léa that the owner had told her that the job had been taken, and that there had been a mistake. In her interview with Nicole Lacelle, Auntie Léa shared the story of what happened next. Auntie Léa was furious Hélène had not been given the job, and she used her anger to lambaste the boss.

> I called him and spoke in Yiddish. "Haven't you heard of Hitler?" "What's that got to do with it?" "I sent you our most competent draper and it's up to you to accept her." "She's Black, she won't fit into my shop." "Listen sir, Hitler

is in power today because Jews like you have left the door open to racism. You won't get another draper, it's Hélène or no one."

So, he calls Shane [Bernard Shane], the person who headed the ILGWU in Montreal], and Shane comes to see me, brings up the same arguments, and I repeat mine. [Then] he calls the boss and tries to convince him to give Hélène a chance: "You know, I've got a Calamity Jane in my office!," talking about me[21]. The boss still refuses. But the next day, he calls; now he agrees to Hélène. I told him he didn't deserve her! That's how Hélène got the job. And he had no trouble at all because of her; it was him, that bastard, who had a problem. When you're part of a minority, you should never forget it. It was damn racism. Rooted in an ignorant mind (Lacelle and Roback, 2005, pp. 142–143).

Auntie Léa's commitment to the principles of seniority and her courage to name and confront racism ensured Hélène was given the position she deserved. In an interview with Sophie Bissonnette, a year or two later, Auntie Léa told the same story of her confrontation with the boss who didn't want to hire Hélène, but this time she provided an unexpected ending to the story.

He [the factory boss], called me a few months later: "Ah, she's fantastic!" He had the nerve to tell me that it wasn't him who was against her, it was the workers. Do you see there... the way out? It wasn't the workers! (*Racism in the Dressmaking Industry (1937–1939)*, 2023)

As discussed in Chapter 5, Auntie Léa would pursue her commitment against racism several decades later in the 1980s by joining the political struggle against apartheid in South Africa. Apartheid, which was in place between 1948 and 1994, was the name given to the racial segregation established under the all-White government of South Africa.

Leaving the ILGWU

In 1939, Auntie Léa left the International Ladies' Garment Workers' Union. In her interview with Nicole Lacelle, she explains why.

> I worked at the Dressmakers' Union until 1939. Everything we had done in terms of education we could no longer maintain. Activism was fading away. It was still the Depression in 1939, but we were preparing for the war industry. On the men's clothing side, we were already starting to get contracts to make uniforms. But in the Dressmakers' Union, with everything that had happened [financially during the Depression], the workers were afraid of losing their jobs, and the union and the bosses were happy to get rid of the activists (Lacelle and Roback, 2005, pp. 144–145).

At first, I was surprised to read that the union as well as the bosses were happy to "get rid of the activists." After all, it was activists like Auntie Léa who provided extraordinary leadership during the 1937 Dressmakers' Strike. However, in an interview with Sophie Bissonnette, Auntie Léa talked about how the ILGWU leaders in Montreal were selling out to the factory bosses. The local radical activists in the union were a thorn in their side. Auntie Léa also talked about how the American leaders of the ILGWU were eager to remove the militant activists from the union. Like Auntie Léa, Rose Pesotta ended up leaving as well, even though she had held the position of vice-president.

Melanie Leavitt explains that the ILGWU's eagerness to remove militant activists from the union speaks to the chilling effect the Duplessis anti-Communist legislation had on the labour movement and the Left as a whole. In the face of laws such as the Padlock Law, some international unions, such as the ILGWU, were anxious to purge the more radical members/organizers from their ranks (Melanie Leavitt, personal communication, 25 March 2025). As Auntie Léa told Nicole Lacelle about Duplessis' attitude towards the unions, "They were all Communists. To him, everyone who wasn't on his side was a Communist" (Lacelle and Roback, 2005, p.166).

Unionizing the workers at RCA

In 1941, two years after she left the ILGWU, Auntie Léa began working for the Radio Corporation of America (RCA) war/munitions plant located in the neighbourhood of Saint-Henri, in Montreal. The RCA plant in Saint-Henri made radios during the Second World War and Auntie Léa was assigned to different jobs there. Auntie Léa had gone to work at RCA with the specific goal of unionizing the plant for the International Brotherhood of Electrical Workers and the United Electrical Workers. In 1941, an unprecedented number of women workers were working in factories like RCA replacing men who were serving overseas in the Second World War. At the time many Montreal families living in the French Canadian working-class neighbourhood of Saint-Henri were living in poverty. In an interview with Sophie Bissonnette, both Auntie Léa and her friend activist Madeleine Parent, told several stories about what that meant.

Léa Roback

… there was one worker, she had one pair of shoes before going to work at RCA Victor with her sister. To go to church on Sunday morning, she lived on Sainte-Émilie Street, and well… she couldn't go with her sister because she had to wait for her to come back from mass, so she could wear her shoes to go to the next mass.

Madeleine Parent

When I started organizing unions in Saint-Henri in '43 and visited many, many families, the housing reminded me later, somewhat, of the portrait in *Bonheur d'occasion* that Gabrielle Roy left us.[22] It was a bit like that, very run-down, almost no amenities, cold that penetrated and a lot of difficulty getting rid of vermin. And the children played in the streets, the parks weren't equipped back then. So they had a stick and a piece of ice for a puck. And they played in the street. And when the mother came back from the factory, anyway, she had to do the big cleaning and prepare dinner. She couldn't be bothered by the children in the house. So that's how it was lived, but it was very tough and the nights were cold.

Sophie Bissonnette

And many children worked in families?

Madeleine Parent

Many children worked in families. You had one room where you [lived with] several children. If there were two rooms in a house, that was a lot, and we managed as best we could in poverty, in the cold, in misery, really (*Poverty in the Neighbourhood of Saint-Henri (1930 et 1940)*, 2023).

From the very beginning of her work at RCA in 1941, Auntie Léa began organizing to unionize the plant. She told interviewer Nicole Lacelle:

> At the beginning, when I started working, I had all my union leaflets hidden underneath in my bag. On top, I put my Kotex pads because … the security people inside really thought they were kings! So, I came in. "Show your bag!" [the security guard said]. "Listen, you can address me with *vous*, right? I say *vous* to you, so say *vous* to me."[23] "Come on, show your bag!" So, I showed him … I opened my bag, and everyone saw it was full of Kotex pads. Then the guys said to him [the security guard], "Ah huh, you got tricked, huh?" And he let me go up. Since I was very flat-chested, I also hid the flyers in my blouse, and when I passed by the female workers, [I'd say], "Here. Take this, take this for the meeting." When they caught me, they moved me to another department. I practically went through the whole factory (Lacelle and Roback, 2005, p. 147).

When Lacelle heard this, she asked, "You must have developed an extraordinary knowledge of the place?" Auntie Léa responded:

> Ah! My goodness! From the basement to the capacitors upstairs. There, there was a forewoman, a bootlicker. Two were very nice; they knew who I was, but they said, "I'm not allowed, but you all, keep going!" "Certainly! If we win, and we will win, your salaries will increase,

and it will be better for you too." And Florence, a beautiful, beautiful person, kind, turned a blind eye. I went to the bathroom very often because that's where we heard the complaints: "That damn foreman, he's after me again!" "It's not funny, eh? Well, if we stick together, that damn foreman won't get the best of us, and we'll be treated like human beings." "Yes, but…" "But in the end, they came on board" (Lacelle and Roback, 2005, pp. 147–148).

It took Auntie Léa and her team a year of organizing before the first union contract was signed at RCA.

> It took some effort. To organize, eight months. It wasn't easy. The bosses, because of war production, were on a cash-plus regime, making a profit, my girl! And at RCA Victor, they continued to press records, which at that time brought in a big profit. There were 4,000 of us at RCA, most of whom were women doing assembly line work. We were putting little gadgets into a big device. They called it the Wireless 19. Some would solder an aluminum piece, then we had to push it onto a shelf; it was heavy, and we had to lift it. And then we had that damned timer: "Oh well, you made 8 in one hour, in 8 hours, you can make 64." I took my time, and then a guy came [over and asked me in English]: "What's the matter now?" (He didn't speak a word of French.) I told him in English, with a serious look: "Trouble." There were always "troubles" with me … He went to see the foreman, then the superintendent, and they moved me to another place. Eventually, they kicked me out! (Lacelle and Roback, 2005, p. 148)

Although RCA had fired Auntie Léa, they eventually took her back. However, when she returned to work, she no longer worked on the production line. She was given a job in the shipping department.

> I worked in shipping, with the guys, I was the only woman! So, I wore pants because they liked to look at the girls… from underneath … (Lacelle and Roback, 2005, p. 149).

Auntie Léa worked at RCA from 1941 to 1952, but she didn't only work as a factory worker. There was an arrangement in the collective agreement that RCA signed with the union that stipulated Auntie Léa could take unpaid leave to work on union grievances and discuss them with the bosses (Lacelle and Roback, 2005, p. 149). Auntie Léa worked at RCA as a grievance officer until 1952 when Maurice Duplessis, the Premier of Quebec at the time, working in collusion with RCA revoked the union's accreditation, allowing the company to fire all of the union militants.

Given Auntie Léa's experience as a union organizer and grievance officer, Lacelle was interested in knowing if Auntie Léa had ever had any interest in moving up higher in the union hierarchy (like Rose Pesotta). Auntie Léa told her:

> No, that wasn't my style … I've always been with the workers. I saw in some unions, great activists who had lost their minds. I never wanted to be a full-timer. I liked being shoulder to shoulder with the people I worked with … I definitely didn't want to step out of the ranks. Me, telling others what they should do… I would have spent my time telling myself, "But you're not doing it, Léa, what you're telling others to do." I wanted to be able

to say "we" and for it to truly be "we." That's what I liked. And you know what, I don't really like meetings. Those endless talks that full-timers have to endure! But with all those meetings, when can you actually get work done? I would never have had the patience … (Lacelle and Roback, 2005, p. 150).

After being fired from RCA in 1952, it wasn't easy to find new work. But Auntie Léa persevered and was hired as a sales assistant at Eaton's department store, where she tried to unionize the other sales assistants who had complaints about their working conditions. When Auntie Léa's attempts to start a union were reported to a manager, she was fired. Next, Auntie Léa worked as a library technician at the Montreal Children's Hospital. She also was hired to teach English in a girls' school but had to quit when she refused to follow the school curriculum. Instead, Auntie Léa chose to teach the girls English through conversation, an approach that she thought would be more useful to them. Decades later, Auntie Léa's conversational approach would gain acceptance in the field of English language education as the goal of communicative competence became increasingly important in English as a Second Language curriculum. Finally, Auntie Léa found a job as a programme administrator at the Quebec Society for the Visually Impaired, a job which she kept for ten years. When I first got to know Auntie Léa as a child in the 1960s, that's where she worked, at the Quebec Society for the Visually Impaired. I remember Auntie Léa liked working there because it allowed her to connect people with resources that could improve their everyday lives.

There were other jobs that Auntie Léa would have liked to do, but she wasn't successful in getting hired for them. For example,

Auntie Léa told Sophie Bissonnette she would have liked to work in social services in the Jewish community. She wanted to work in a place that would allow her to care for women. But Jewish social services wouldn't hire her because they thought she was too radical (*An activist looking for employment (1950 and 1960)*, 2023). So, Auntie Léa found other ways to support women. She continued to participate in many social movements in Montreal, including access to legalized abortion and contraception, access to housing, anti-racism in Canada, and anti-apartheid in South Africa. She also supported equity in education and pay equity, protested against the Vietnam War, and defended the rights of immigrant and Indigenous women. Much of this political work took place with an organization called *La Voix des Femmes/Voice of Women*. A discussion of Auntie Léa's work with Voice of Women also appears in the next chapter.

Sophie Bissonnette remembers Auntie Léa as a constant presence in protests and marches, passing out leaflets and lending her respected voice to a variety of causes. In the last scene of her 1991 film about Auntie Léa's social justice work, Bissonnette shows Auntie Léa, in her late 80s standing in front of Steinberg's, a supermarket in her neighbourhood of Côte des Neiges, in the middle of winter, handing out flyers about the violence of war toys. "There's nothing that I like better," Auntie Léa says in the scene, "than to be standing on a street corner, passing out leaflets because this is how you come to understand what people are about" (*Des lumières dans la grande noirceur*, 1991).

Age and cold winter conditions didn't deter Auntie Léa from her activism. At the age of 85, she demonstrated with thousands of young women in Quebec City to defend a woman's right to abortion in L'Affaire Chantal Daigle (discussed in the next chapter). At the age of 91, she was still working on the front lines as she led the *Marche du pain et roses* (the Bread and Roses March), an important initiative against poverty organized by the Federation des femmes du Québec in 1996.

Auntie Léa's work for workers' rights in Quebec in the 1930s and 1940s and her work for women's rights and peace in the 1960s, 1970s, 1980s, and 1990s earned her much recognition. A discussion of the honours she received in her life takes place in Chapter 6. In the next chapter, however, I share stories about Auntie Léa's suffrage work with Thérèse Casgrain to win the right for women to vote in Quebec. The chapter continues with stories about her post-suffrage peace movement work with Voice of Women and her activism to legalize abortion.

5
Montreal

Fighting for women's rights (1933–2000)

> …I always, always worked with the aim of helping … After all, I was a woman. And women needed a lot of support. And especially on the issue of abortion, and injustices. So that was always in me. And that, doesn't go away.
>
> – Léa Roback[24]

***

In 1936, Auntie Léa was recruited by suffragist Thérèse Casgrain who wanted her to join the women's suffrage movement in Quebec. Casgrain had heard about Auntie Léa's successful union work in the dressmaking industry and needed her help in recruiting working-class women to the movement. Auntie Léa liked Thérèse Casgrain very much. In an interview with journalist Susan Schwartz, she said:

> Madame Casgrain was a terrific woman. She lived on Elm Avenue in a beautiful home, but you know, she wasn't the kind who had it written all over her that she was a

wealthy woman. She was also dressed very simple, and she was sympatico.

It didn't matter if you had an apron on or your hair wasn't just so. If she felt you were honest and sincere, she wanted you to work with her. And we did. We rang doorbells, tried to talk to women …

We learned that the best time to go was in the afternoon when the husbands weren't there. [In the evenings] the husband would be in the kitchen reading his newspaper. "Who is it?" he would ask. "A woman who wants to know if I want to vote." "Close the door," the husband would say (Schwartz and Roback, 1997, pp. 7–8).

The right to vote

In Canada, women won the right to vote sporadically. For example, White women from the province of Manitoba became the first to vote provincially in 1916. Two years later, in 1918, White women and Métis women across Canada were granted the right to vote federally. However, it wasn't until decades later that First Nations and Inuit peoples, as well as most Canadians of Asian descent could vote federally. First Nations peoples could not vote federally until 1960 because under the *Indian Act,* they were seen as incapable of managing their own affairs or voting. Inuit peoples were given the right to vote at the federal level ten years earlier in 1950, when the Canadian government decided that they were distinct from First Nations peoples. Asian Canadians weren't given the right to vote until 1948.[25]

In 1936, the year that Thérèse Casgrain recruited Auntie Léa to work for women's suffrage, no women in Quebec were able to vote provincially. The provincial government made decisions about education and other family issues, and Casgrain believed it was imperative that women in Quebec had a say on them. She had become the president of *La Ligue des droits de la femme* / The League for Women's Rights in 1928, eight years before she recruited Auntie Léa. Each year the League would find a member of the Quebec Parliament to sponsor a suffrage bill. Each year, the bill was rejected. In an interview with Ghila Bénesty-Sroka, Auntie Léa said this about her work with Thérèse Casgrain:

> We struggled a lot, there were endless meetings. Taschereau [the Premier of Quebec between 1920–1936] was against women's right to vote. "They come to show us their hats," he said (Bénesty-Sroka, 1996, p. 84).

The dismissive remark demonstrates how difficult it was for the League to have their demand for the right to vote taken seriously. Gaining the right to vote took decades and, in the end, was the result of activism undertaken by a coalition of several groups particularly: *La Ligue des droits de la femme* / The League of Women's Rights, led by Thérèse Casgrain; *La Fédération Nationale Saint-Jean Baptiste,* led by Marie Lacoste Gérin-Lajoie) *L'Alliance canadienne pour le vote des femmes au Québec/* Canadian Alliance for Women's Vote in Québec, led by Idola Saint-Jean, Anna Marks-Lyman and Carrie Derrick.[26]

While Auntie Léa respected Thérèse Casgrain, she believed that the middle class and wealthy women involved in The League of Women's Rights did not understand the everyday struggles of Quebec's working-class women in the 1930s. They had never visited working-class neighbourhoods or homes. As Auntie Léa explained to interviewer Andrée Pomerleau:

> At the time, the primary struggle for working women was the struggle to put food on the table, the struggle to make ends meet with nothing (Pomerleau and Roback, n.d. p. 10).

Auntie Léa tried to build bridges between the feminist and union movements by bringing the issues of working-class women into the bourgeois feminist movement of the time. For example, during the ILGWU's campaign to recruit workers and in the lead-up to the strike (from fall 1936 and through to the strike), the union forged strong ties with both Thérèse Casgrain and Idola Saint-Jean, inviting the women to come and speak to the workers at union meetings, rallies, and even speaking to the gathered workers during the Dressmakers' Strike. This relationship was particularly valuable to advancing the suffrage movement, since it provided the movement with direct access to working-class French Catholic women. The Quebec suffrage movement had long faced the challenge of successfully reaching and including the francophone, Catholic working-class, and was often perceived as being a middle-class movement of the bourgeoisie.

The coalition of suffragist groups used a variety of strategies to mobilize Quebec women in the fight to win the right to vote. They organized demonstrations and marches, and urged women to sign petitions and write to the provincial government. Every year a delegation of women from a variety of suffrage groups, most predominantly from the League of Women's Rights would go to Quebec City to demand that the National Assembly give women the right to vote. Thérèse Casgrain used her popular national radio show on Radio-Canada, which focused on women's issues, to discuss the importance of winning the right to vote. In 1929, Idola Saint-Jean published a series of bilingual articles in *The Montreal Herald*.

The story of how women in Quebec finally won the right to vote in 1940 – four years after Auntie Léa joined the movement – began with the provincial election of 1939. After Maurice Duplessis [the Premier of Quebec at the time] called a surprise general election, Quebec suffragists immediately launched a new publicity campaign on the radio, in the press, and in letters to the candidates. The League of Women's Rights and the Canadian Alliance for Women's Vote in Québec resolutely supported the Liberal Party which had finally placed women's suffrage on its program after much lobbying from the suffragists (Casgrain, 1972, p. 91).[27]

Maurice Duplessis and Union Nationale had been in power since 1936 and were expected to win the 1939 election. Instead, the Liberal Party won, and Casgrain was hopeful that it wouldn't be long before women would finally be given the right to vote. However, when the new Liberal Premier Adélard Godbout came into office, he didn't immediately declare his intentions about women's right to vote. To remind Godbout of the Liberal Party's promise, Casgrain encouraged women to write to the Premier and demand he honour his commitment to suffrage. Letters, telegrams, and petitions poured in from all corners of the province (Casgrain, 1972, p. 91). On 20 February 1940, the women's suffrage bill was included in Godbout's Speech from the Throne.

However, the next challenge was to ensure that the bill passed. Casgrain explains:

> The anti-suffragettes,[28] both men and women, who were particularly numerous in the rural areas and had been content until then to express their opinions moderately, suddenly realized that we had government support and redoubled the violence of their attacks. Right from the beginning they had been supported by our clergy …
>
> …on the 7th of March, sixteen days after the Throne Speech, there was great excitement throughout the province. An official [anti-suffragette] communique from the highest ecclesiastical authority, His Eminence Rodrigue Cardinal Villeneuve, was published in *La Semaine religieuse* (Casgrain, 1972, p. 92).

In the end, two decades of political struggle for the right to vote by several groups of committed women finally paid off. On 9 April 1940, Bill No. 18 was introduced in the Legislative Assembly. The bill was passed on 18 April 1940, and was adopted into law on 25 April 1940. The importance of women being granted the right to vote was never underestimated by the suffragists. As Auntie Léa told Nicole Lacelle, "It wasn't only the right to vote that was at stake, but all the doors the vote would open for women" (Lacelle and Roback, 2005, p. 160).

La Voix des Femmes/Voice of Women (VOW) and peace activism

Established in 1960, not long after the beginning of the Cold War, *La Voix des Femmes*/Voice of Women (VOW) is Canada's oldest national feminist peace group. Their mission is to build cultures of peace through education and advocacy (Macpherson and de Bruin, 2020). As discussed in Chapter 3, the Cold War took place between the end of the Second World War and the collapse of the Soviet Union in 1991. During this time, the world was largely divided into two ideological camps — the United States-led capitalist "West" and the Soviet-dominated communist "East." Canada aligned with the West (Herd, 2006). In 1960, increasing tensions between the United States and the Soviet Union led to fears of nuclear war. The American government had begun developing and testing atomic weapons (nearly 200 between 1945 and 1958), and many Canadians, who shared a border with the United States, became concerned about nuclear radiation (Strong-Boag, 2016). Their concerns led to the creation of groups devoted to peace and disarmament, including VOW. The Canadian government's acceptance of the use of Bomarc missiles (with their potential nuclear warheads) also pushed women to join the organization. The CIM-10B Bomarc was the world's first long-range, nuclear-capable, ground-to-air anti-aircraft missile. Two squadrons of the missile were purchased and deployed by the Canadian government in 1958 as part of Canada's role during the Cold War (Boyko, 2021).

Thérèse Casgrain founded the Quebec chapter of VOW in 1961 (Strong-Boag, 2016). Auntie Léa joined that same year. During the 40 years Auntie Léa was part of VOW, the group not only campaigned and lobbied all levels of government against the proliferation of nuclear weapons and for disarmament, it also protested the Vietnam War, apartheid in South Africa, and demonstrated for environmental protection and access to abortion. VOW also fought against pornography which it believed was responsible for violence against women.

Over sixty years since its founding in 1960, VOW continues to organize extensive educational campaigns, lobby governments, hold meetings and conferences, and send representatives to other countries to address mutual concerns of women internationally and promote action. For example, in 2000, VOW was part of an international alliance that successfully pressed for adoption of Security Council Resolution 1325 on women, peace and security. The resolution called for the increased participation of women in peace and security efforts and measures to protect women and girls from gender-based violence during armed conflict (Macpherson and de Bruin, 2020).

Auntie Léa was a constant presence at Voice of Women meetings, demonstrations and events. In 1982, at the age of 79, she was interviewed by VOW for one of their publications. Auntie Léa took the opportunity to discuss an early project undertaken by Voice of Women: the 1962–1963 Milk Teeth Campaign, which examined the impact of nuclear weapons testing. She explained:

> At that time, Ursula Franklin, a scientist working with *La Voix*, informed us that the level of strontium-90—a radioactive residue produced by nuclear weapons testing—could be detected by analyzing children's baby teeth. We wanted to determine if the population was being exposed to higher levels of radiation since the widespread nuclear weapons testing began in 1952. That's how we started our campaign, in collaboration with other groups around the world, to push for a treaty banning nuclear tests.

> We distributed thousands of brochures, visited stores and schools, and most importantly, we spoke to women, trying to explain what we wanted to do with their children's teeth. The response was incredible. Teeth came pouring in by the thousands from all corners of Canada. The results were conclusive. Our analyses showed that the population was absorbing increasing amounts of strontium-90 since the onset of nuclear testing … (Voice of Women, 1982, p. 3).

Strontium-90 is considered by medical researchers and doctors to be a cancer-causing substance because it damages the genetic material (DNA) in cells. Its increased presence in children's teeth was cause for serious concern.

Like Auntie Léa, my cousin Judith Roback also attended protests against nuclear weapons testing and the dangers of Strontium-90. In one of our email exchanges, Judith shared a song she learned while marching at one of these protests. It was called Strontium-90, and it had three verses and a chorus (Judith Roback, personal communication, 24 November 2024).

Strontium 90
Verse 1
Last night I went to a party.
Danced and I just about passed out!
But just when the party was at its gayest
Some crazy guy began to shout:

Chorus
Strontium, strontium, strontium 90
Fall out will get you even underground

Strontium, strontium, strontium 90

Now if you want some strontium, strontium 90

There's enough to go around.

Verse 2

What will we get from radiation?

No neck, two necks, maybe three.

Each one will have his own mutation.

Nobody else will look like me.

Chorus

Verse 3

So drink to the course of evolution

The next one may very well be you

Keep clouding the air with pollution and

We'll see you next year at the zoo.

Chorus (Cleary and Clearly, 1959)[29]

The risks and dangers around nuclear armament continue to this day. While during the 1990s there were positive moves towards nuclear disarmament among the major nuclear power states, mainly due to the end of the Cold War following the fall of the Berlin Wall in November 1989, a reverse trend has emerged within some smaller nations. For example, after the Gulf War in 1991, in which Iraq was defeated by the coalition forces led by the United States military, North Korea and Iran began developing nuclear weapons as a deterrent to the US. In 1993 North Korea withdrew from the Treaty on the Non-Proliferation of Nuclear Weapons (the NPT) and tested its first intermediate-range missile, Nodon 1. In 2009, it produced an intercontinental ballistic missile (ICBM).

Similarly, after the Gulf War, Iran strengthened its desire to produce weapons-grade plutonium and has pursued this goal ever since (Nasu and Nishimura, 2019). It is important to note that during the Gulf War, the coalition forces led by the United States (US) used 950,000 depleted uranium bullets (about 300 tons), which later caused symptoms similar to those caused by radiation among American soldiers (Nasu and Nishimura, 2019).

I learned about the impact of radiation exposure, as well as the horrifying and devastating impact of the Atomic Bomb dropped by the US military on the Japanese city of Hiroshima on 6 August 1945, when I visited the Hiroshima Peace Memorial Museum. At the museum gift shop, I bought a book called *Hiroshima: A Tragedy Never to Be Repeated* written by Masamoto Nasu and illustrated by Shigeo Nishimura. The book describes the historical background of the production of the A-bomb that was dropped on Hiroshima and the effects of the bomb. In the book Nasu writes about the bombing this way:

> *Hibakusha* (victims of the A-bomb) call the atomic bomb *pika-don*, meaning "flash-bang" which refers to the sudden bright flash and the deafening blast that engulfed them immediately after the bomb exploded. People close to the hypocenter say they saw an orange-coloured flash; those who were further away saw a blue-white color. The "flash-bang" was accompanied by extraordinary levels of heat and radiation …
>
> … Immediately after the flash a violent wind engulfed the city, knocking down everything in its path. All the buildings near the hypocenter, with the exception of a few earth-quake-resistant structures, were destroyed.

Wooden houses were smashed to pieces. Large trees were uprooted and blown around in the wind like paper. People, too, were tossed about mercilessly …

… For a while, those who were not killed instantly could not even cry out. Several minutes later spot fires broke out, making Hiroshima appear like a scene from hell. None of the victims of this first atomic bomb had any idea of what had happened. Most just thought that a regular bomb had exploded very close by. But as people ran through the flames trying to escape, they realized this was like nothing they had known before. No matter where they went, the entire city was destroyed. The dead and injured were everywhere (Nasu and Nishimura, 2019, pp. 24–33).

After the explosion, Nasu writes, the temperature of the area immediately around the hypocenter soared to 3,000–4,000 degrees Celsius due to the heat of the thermal rays emitted by the fireball created by the explosion. The radiation caused by the explosion was not just the initial radiation emitted at the time of the blast. The soil on the ground, building materials and many other substances exposed to the blast absorbed the radiation and continued to emit it over a long period of time. The damage caused by the bomb was the result of a combination of thermal rays, the actual blast, and radioactivity (Nasu and Nishimura, 2019).

Nasu estimates that there were approximately 350,000 people in Hiroshima on the morning of the blast on 6 August 1945. However, the number of radiation victims was far greater because after the bomb was dropped, people from outside the city came to Hiroshima to look for relatives and friends who were injured or killed by the blast. Medical teams came to help the victims and others came to arrange mass cremations. Still others began the task of cleaning up the city. Many of these people were also affected by radiation. People who remained outside the city were affected by radioactive "black rain" which came down after the blast.

Altogether, Nasu estimates an additional 100,000 people were irradiated by the A-bomb, for a total of 450,000 people (Nasu and Nishimura, 2019, p. 48). The first symptoms of radiation included the loss of hair, bloody faeces, intense nausea and vomiting, accompanied by general lethargy. These were followed by a lack of appetite, fever, violent diarrhoea with bloody faeces and bleeding into the skin. Most of the people who had these symptoms died within ten days. People who survived the first symptoms subsequently suffered from keloids (thick raised, often painful, scars that occur in places where skin has been injured), cataracts, aplastic anaemia, acute leukaemia, miscarriage, birth defects and many types of cancer (Nasu and Nishimura, 2019).

Nasu and Nishimura conclude their book about the devastating death toll and horrific and long-lasting effects of the A-bomb with just one sentence: "It is the duty of everyone alive today to ensure that what happened in Hiroshima on that fateful day is not forgotten and is never repeated" (p. 69). It is a thought that became the foundation of the anti-nuclear movement post-World War Two, and the foundation of the work undertaken by Voice of Women in Canada. Unfortunately, as discussed earlier, since the 1990s there has been less political commitment to nuclear disarmament. However, as I write this chapter in November 2024, the

American-Russian nuclear arms control treaty, known as the New START treaty, has been extended until 5 February 2026. As well, civil movements against nuclear weapons continue to be active. If Auntie Léa were alive today, she would no doubt be involved in the anti-nuclear movement in Canada through Voice of Women. She would be working hard to create a world where people would be protected from the dangers of irradiation and mass destruction.

Fighting for the right to abortion

In addition to contributing to anti-nuclear activist work, Auntie Léa was also involved in efforts to legalize abortion in the 1960s, 1970s, and 1980s. Her activism around the right to abortion actually began decades earlier when she supported women workers with unwanted pregnancies. In the 1930s and 1940s pregnancies outside of marriage were socially condemned in Quebec and Canada. At the time, the Canadian Criminal Code prohibited the distribution of contraceptive information or materials and the performance of abortions. Under these conditions, when single Catholic women became pregnant, they had two choices: give birth secretly at the Miséricorde Hospital, a hospital run by the Miséricorde nuns or have an illegal abortion. Abortions were mostly done by either an untrained abortionist or by rare doctors who agreed to perform them at the risk of being arrested and prosecuted. Some of the doctors who would perform abortions were English-speaking Jewish doctors that Auntie Léa knew. Sitting on the border between English, French, Jewish, and Catholic communities in Montreal, Auntie Léa was able to provide care that otherwise would not have been available to the women she worked with.

Babies delivered at the Miséricorde hospital were placed in orphanages temporarily until their mothers took them back or put them up for adoption. However, as historian Denyse Baillairgeon writes, "a staggering number of them died from a lack of adequate care" (*Unwanted Pregnancies*, 2023). In an interview with Sophie Bissonnette, Auntie Léa shared a story about a worker named Céline who needed support.

> There was one particular case, a pregnant woman who was too far along to have an abortion. So, she went to the Miséricorde [Hospital]. At that time, it wasn't a very welcoming place. She went there, and the women there weren't allowed to smoke. But they had always smoked! And they weren't allowed to gossip, and they had to atone for their sins. Oh, so many sins! Mortal sins! This sin! That sin!
>
> So, I went with her. And one day she said to me, "Get me out of here. I'm going to die if I stay here." And she was pregnant. Very pregnant. But she said, "Get me out of here!" So, I did. But where could I take her? There was the Salvation Army, and they were always happy to convert Catholics to Protestantism. So I spoke to Major . . . I don't remember her name, but she was at the Catherine-Booth Hospital in Notre-Dame-de-Grâce, which nowadays is no longer a maternity hospital, but a hospital for people with disabilities. So, she said, "Sure, we'll look after her."
>
> And I had spoken to . . . At the time, there was a Doctor Letondale. I said, "She has to get out of here." And he said, "I'm a doctor," —he was a gynecologist and an obstetrician— "I can't help you with that." So I said, "I'm going

> to get this done!" And the head nun—I think her name was Sister Parent, I'm not sure. She was a very dignified woman. I told her, "I want her out of here." "Oh, you can't take her. She's a sinner. And she'll have her baby here." And I said, "She can't stay here. I'm taking her with me." So, she looked at me, and she said, "You're not Catholic, are you?" I said, "No ma'am, I'm Jewish," but [more importantly,] "I'm human." So, there was a bit of a discussion. And she was smart enough to understand that I was going to keep at her until I got the woman—whose name was Céline— out of there. So . . . At the time we didn't take taxis. We took the streetcar. So, we went there, and an extraordinary doctor named Dr. McCaffrey, an Irishman, examined her properly, and said, "You know she's got twins! Twins!" (*Unwanted Pregnancies,* 2023)

Céline worked for the Salvation Army, cleaning, sweeping, dusting until she went into labour. The delivery went well, and after the babies were born, Céline and Auntie Léa needed to find a place for the twins. Because Céline was Catholic, she wanted a Catholic place. Auntie Léa found one.

> So, there was a place. Oh, goodness. There were nurseries in Pointe-aux Trembles, and in Saint-Laurent also, I think. Places like that. So, we went . . . She was carrying one of the babies, and I was carrying the other. It was really very moving. Getting to Pointe-aux Trembles was quite a voyage in those days. They were very welcoming there, but when we went upstairs and she showed us the place, it was like . . . I said, "There must be five hundred of them." I don't know how many—a huge number of little cradles, all these little cribs and little babies. Because

remember, there was a lot of prostitution here, and there were also unmarried women who gave birth, and they had nothing, so the babies ended up . . . The children needed a place to stay, so that's where they went. So they did what they could, and we went to visit them for the next three Sundays. And on the third Sunday, they were already "angels in Heaven who will pray for you" (*Unwanted Pregnancies,* 2023).

To clarify, Bissonnette asked Auntie Léa if the babies had died. Auntie Léa replied:

Yes. But I can't blame them. You should have seen the place. Row upon row. It smelled like urine in there. There were maybe one or two nuns in there from time to time. But how could they take care of that many babies? It wasn't their fault. But it was good that they believed they were "angels in Heaven" who would pray for their mother, who no longer had anything to worry about. And those women . . .There were some who said that later, they would go get their babies. Like Céline. That's what she had wanted to do. She later got married. She had one baby with her husband. Very good. I used to hear from her regularly during the holidays, but now, I don't even know if she's still alive (*Unwanted Pregnancies,* 2023).

Auntie Léa's story of how she helped Céline leave La Miséricorde hospital, find a doctor who could deliver her babies safely, and then find a Catholic place to care for her twin babies demonstrates the broad range of ways in which her activism was characterized by care. Auntie Léa cared for Céline without the shame or judgement Céline experienced at La Miséricorde hospital.

Auntie Léa also cared for the women workers who wanted an illegal abortion.

> Well, kitchen table abortions, those were, I wanted nothing to do with those. I ... Like I said, when I worked at RCA Victor, for example, there were a lot of questions. And when I worked in dressmaking, there were safe places you could go, with real doctors, in clinics, and those people didn't lose babies ... But you needed money to get an abortion there. And there were other places to get an abortion, all over the place. Safe places, as though you were in a hospital. They were all over town ... And I went with the patients, and I saw how they cleaned their instruments, and I saw their gloves, and I saw if they had washed their hands properly. Women don't get abortions just for fun, do they? (*Unwanted Pregnancies,* 2023).

When she was working on the lines at the RCA Victor plant, Auntie Léa tried to support young women who came to her needing abortions. But she wasn't always successful. In an interview with writer Susan Schwartz about why, at the age of 85, she was participating in a right to abortion march Auntie Léa talked about two young women she knew who had died from botched abortions.

> One was only in her early twenties, perhaps 21. She couldn't tell her family. If you became pregnant, it was like being a streetwalker. There were doctors who would do abortions. Good doctors, not women who did abortions on the kitchen table. But this route cost money. One [doctor] had told this girl it would cost $200. Instead, she went to a woman on Parthenais Street who did it for

> $50. I don't have to go into the details. Soon afterward, she started hemorrhaging. She went to St. Luc Hospital but died within eight hours. Another abortion was done with a different method, but the result was the same (Schwartz and Roback, 1996/1997, p. 9).

As a witness to two deaths from abortion, the right to abortion by making it legal was an issue close to Auntie Léa's heart. She told Schwartz:

> I'm just one woman and I saw two deaths [due to illegal abortions]. That's why I'm involved. I'm not going to sit here and contemplate my navel. I'll have lots of time to do nothing when they put me in a box and close the lid (Schwartz and Roback, 1996/1997, p. 9).

In Canada, abortion was illegal until 1969 when following pressure from the feminist movement (in Quebec women mobilized under several different coalitions which fought for access to free abortions) an amendment to the Criminal Law Act legalized therapeutic abortions, as long as they were only performed in accredited hospitals with proper approval from the hospital's Therapeutic Abortion Committee (TAC). Each TAC would consist of a committee of doctors who could certify that continuing a pregnancy would likely endanger a woman's life or health. Abortions performed outside accredited hospitals without the approval of a Therapeutic Abortion Committee were still illegal (Long, 2006).

The interpretation of the 1969 law varied widely among doctors and hospitals, leading to uneven access to abortion. The criteria for abortion were the physical or mental well-being of the woman, which was decided by each hospital's TAC. However, there was no requirement for a hospital to establish a TAC. In the early 1980s, only about one-third of hospitals across the country had one. Some committees took a liberal stance and allowed most requests, while others blocked almost all requests. Access to legal abortions was easier in major metropolitan areas, but much harder outside large cities. For example, in the province of Prince Edward Island, when the sole Therapeutic Abortion Committee shut down in 1982, legal abortions were no longer available in the province.[30]

In Quebec, a 1977 report by the *Comité de lutte pour l'avortement et la contraception libres et gratuities* (the Committee for the Fight for Free and Accessible Abortion and Contraception) estimated between 10,000 and 25,000 women in Quebec would have an illegal abortion that year. This statistic reflects the continued lack of access to abortions in hospitals in Quebec at the time (Melanie Leavitt, personal communication, 25 March 2025).

The TACs often took days or weeks to make their decisions, pushing a pregnancy further along than it would have been otherwise. If a TAC chose not to see a woman who wanted an abortion, she did not have the right to appeal the TAC's decision. Advocates for access to abortion rights like Auntie Léa believed that the choice should be made by women themselves, rather than a panel of doctors.

In 1983, to advocate for the legalization of abortion outside accredited hospitals three doctors, Drs. Henry Morgentaler, Leslie Frank Smoling and Robert Scott, set up an abortion clinic in Toronto to perform abortions on women who had not received certification from a TAC. The clinic brought public attention to the reality that abortion was still illegal and frequently inaccessible unless it was performed in an accredited hospital with the approval of a TAC. The doctors argued that women should have complete control over the decision on whether to have an abortion (Long, 2006).

Before his work in Toronto, in the 1970s, Dr. Morgentaler and other women's health groups in the Quebec feminist movement, such as *Le Centre de santé des femmes* were defying the law and performing safe abortions in their clinics in Montreal. Their work both addressed women's needs for an abortion and advocated for women's right to choose.

The political advocacy of Drs. Morgentaler, Smoling and Scott was supported by feminist organizations including the Voice of Women. It was also supported by several national organizations such as the Canadian Abortion Rights Action League (CARAL), Canadians for Choice, and the Pro-Choice Action Network. When CARAL folded it was replaced by the Abortion Rights Coalition of Canada.

In 1988, the Supreme Court of Canada ruled in R. v. Morgentaler that the existing 1969 law was unconstitutional and struck it down. The ruling found that the law violated a woman's right to "life, liberty and security of the person" guaranteed under the Canadian Charter of Rights and Freedoms established in 1982. Since the 1988 ruling, there have been no criminal laws regulating abortion in Canada. However, some provinces restrict access to abortion in various ways that do not criminalize it (Long, 2006).

In Quebec, there was another legal case related to abortion that was important to Voice of Women. In 1989, a year after the 1988 ruling that decriminalized abortion, a Quebec woman named Chantale Daigle was prevented from having an abortion, by her former boyfriend Jean-Guy Tremblay who obtained a restraining order against her doing so. Tremblay argued that he was protecting the rights of the foetus. The case went to the Supreme Court of Canada, which found a foetus has no legal status in Canada as a person, either in Canada or Quebec. This meant that men who state they are protecting fetal rights cannot acquire injunctions to stop their partners from obtaining abortions in Canada. In other words, the Supreme Court of Canada ruled that only a woman could make the choice to have an abortion; a man had no legal say in a woman's choice to terminate a pregnancy or carry it to completion (Long, 2006).[31]

Sixteen years later, in July 2015, after a lengthy review process, the Canadian government permitted doctors to begin prescribing Mifegymiso, a drug regimen that allows women to end an early pregnancy (within 49 days of becoming pregnant) at home. Designed in part to improve women's access to abortion, the drugs act by inducing a miscarriage. While in some provinces, the government requires doctors to dispense Mifegymiso directly to patients, rather than giving them a prescription they can fill at a pharmacy, in Quebec, women can get the drug at a pharmacy, and it is now covered by the Quebec health plan (Long, 2006). Auntie Léa would be delighted.

Fighting against pornography and violence against women

Another issue Auntie Léa was involved in as a member of Voice of Women was the fight against pornography. In her VOW interview, Auntie Léa explained that she understood pornography to be a form of violence against both women and men. She was also concerned about the women who were exploited in the pornography industry. As discussed in Chapter 4, Auntie Léa spent years fighting sexual harassment and abuse in the factories she helped unionize. She told her VOW interviewer:

> Right now, I'm also very active in the fight against pornography. That is violence—not just against women. It's also a form of violence against the men who watch it. As you know, it's unemployed women who are exploited in this way, and we can guess who's making the money at the end of the line. The issues of pornography and militarization are linked; they are part of the same phenomenon (Voice of Women, 1982, p. 3).

In the last 50 years, a multitude of views on pornography have emerged in feminist writing. These views range from total condemnation of pornography as an act of violence against women to an embracing of (some) pornography as a means of feminist expression. Often these views have been connected to the authors' perspectives on sexuality, sex work, and BDSM (bondage and discipline, dominance and submission, and sadomasochism).

In 1981, Canadian filmmaker Bonnie Sherr Klein (writer Naomi Klein's mother) directed a documentary called *Not a Love Story* which shared many of the perspectives on pornography that were circulating at the time (Klein, 1981). In the film, produced by the National Film Board of Canada, Klein and journalist Lindalee Tracey talked to porn actors and sex workers about their work. They also spoke to several anti-pornography and sex-positive feminists. Reflecting the political differences and tensions in feminist thinking about pornography at the time, the National Film Board of Canada was publicly criticized for making a film on the subject. And the Ontario Board of Censors, because of the film's pornographic content, banned it (Wise, 2014).

Auntie Léa believed pornography encouraged violence against women. The writings of anti-pornography feminists such as Andrea Dworkin (e.g., Dworkin, 1981), Catharine McKinnon (e.g., Dworkin and MacKinnon, 1988), and Robin Morgan (e.g., 1978) would have resonated with her. More recent writings by journalist Robert Jensen around the ways pornography and militarization are linked (Jensen, 2010) would also have resonated with her.

Robert Jensen writes that pornography and militarization can be linked through the idea that in the patriarchal world we live in, men are socialized to pursue dominance through aggression and violence. In his public talks with young men, including young men in the military, Jensen explains that sex in pornography is often violent and based on domination and submission — male domination and female submission. Pornography sexualizes domination and submission. It makes male dominance sexy. Serving in the military is also based on domination through aggression and violence, in the service of deepening and extending elite control over the resources and markets in the world (Jensen, 2010).

While I believe Dworkin, MacKinnon, and Morgan's work, along with Jensen, would have been aligned with Auntie Léa's ideas about pornography, it is important to point out that many feminist writers at the time – regardless of their views on pornography – were opposed to the censorship of pornography. They argued that censorship had never reduced violence against women, but it had been used to silence women and derail efforts for social change. For example, the American organization Feminists for Free Expression, founded by Marcia Pally in 1992, pointed to several instances of censorship that had done exactly that (Wikipedia, n.d.). The censorship of the writing on birth control by Margaret Sanger, the feminist plays of Holly Hughes, the women's health book *Our Bodies Ourselves* by the Boston Health Collective (a book that I consulted frequently in my twenties), and the lesbian novel *The Well of Loneliness* by Radcliffe Hall all silenced women writers on issues that were important to women: contraception, abortion, and sexuality.

Around the same time in Canada, Little Sister's Book and Art Emporium, an independent bookstore in Vancouver which sold gay and lesbian books, also experienced the consequences of censorship when they began having difficulty receiving books they had ordered from the United States. Many of the books they had ordered were classified as "obscene" by Canada Customs and were refused entry into the country. Little Sister's went to court to challenge the provision of the *Customs Act* which prohibited the importation of obscene material. They also challenged the section of the Act that put the onus on the importer (the bookstore) to disprove obscenity.

The court challenge went all the way to the Supreme Court of Canada. The Court ruled that Canadian Customs had indeed targeted shipments to the bookstore and attempted to prevent their entry into Canada. Consequently, the government was found to have violated section 2 of the Canadian Charter of Rights and Freedoms. However, the violation was justified under section 1 of the Charter. While the law itself was saved, the Supreme Court concluded that the way the law was implemented by customs officials was discriminatory and should be remedied. The Supreme Court also struck down part of the law that put the responsibility on an importer (importers like Little Sister's) to prove material was not obscene. While the ruling upheld Canada Customs' right to prevent the importation of material that had already been banned as obscene by the courts, it curtailed the agency's right to pre-emptively or punitively detain material that had not been banned (Fuller and Black, 2000).

A documentary film about Little Sister's legal struggle, called *Little Sister's vs. Big Brother* was released in 2002 (Homeboys Productions Ltd., 2018). Directed by filmmaker Aerlyn Weissman the film documented the 15-year legal battle between Little Sister's and the courts. Weissman was able to capture the moment when Canadian policymakers were told they had to rewrite the country's policy on the classification of obscene material. She was also able to demonstrate how discrimination against gay rights, gay literature, and the suppression of free speech remain issues in the twenty-first century. Indeed, contemporary bans on queer and trans books in many American schools have silenced teachers from educating their students on queer and trans lives and queer and trans human rights. For example, between July 2021 and June 2023, PEN America recorded nearly 10,000 instances of book bans in the United States. These bans spread to 41 out of 52 states in the United States with Florida and Texas having the highest number of bans in the country (PEN America, 2024).

In Canada, to mark the International Transgender Day of Visibility, PEN Canada asked writer S. Bear Bergman address the recent wave of book bans in the United States and the growing threat these bans posed to queer and trans writers. In their response to PEN Canada's request, Bear had this to say:

> In my work – both as a writer on queer and trans topics and as the publisher of Flamingo Rampant which makes racially-diverse, feminist children's books celebrating 2SLGBTQ+ kids, families, and communities – I am constantly concerned with what I have termed "justice of the imagination," the critical responsibility of showing all kids that any kid can be the hero of a story (PEN Canada, 2023).

Like Bear Bergman, I am a writer and publisher of queer and trans books and plays. The argument that queer and trans books and plays are important resonates deeply with me. Unfortunately, I never had the opportunity to talk to Auntie Léa about my queer and trans activism – she died just as I was beginning to bring that work into my teaching, research, and writing. I also never had the opportunity to talk to her about the politics of censoring pornography. However, I believe that if she were alive today, Auntie Léa would fight against book bans, and be a strong ally for queer and trans activists.

Fighting against apartheid

As an intersectional feminist and activist, Auntie Léa had a strong commitment against racism and joined the political struggle against apartheid in South Africa. As mentioned in Chapter 4, apartheid was the name given to the racial segregation that was established under the all-White government in South Africa between 1948 and 1994. Apartheid dictated that non-White South Africans – the majority of the population – were required to live in separate areas from Whites. They were also required to use separate public facilities.

One of the leaders of the anti-apartheid movement in South Africa was Nelson Mandela (1918–2013). Mandela was imprisoned for 24 years for his activist work and became a symbol of the struggle against apartheid in South Africa. When he was finally released in 1990, anti-apartheid activists worldwide rejoiced. Four years later, Mandela became South Africa's first Black president. He served as president until 1999, and his government took on the responsibility of both dismantling the legacy of apartheid and working towards racial reconciliation (Nelson Mandela Foundation, 2024).

When Auntie Léa died in August 2000, I received several of her books. One of these books was an anthology called *For Nelson Mandela* (Derrida and Tlili, 1987). The book, published before Mandela was released from prison, contained 23 pieces of writing in honour of Mandela. Like some of the other books I inherited from Auntie Léa, there were newspaper articles folded up and tucked inside the book. The articles were about Nelson Mandela and his struggle against apartheid in South Africa. In several of the articles, Auntie Léa had underlined particular sentences, and written comments in the margins. Her underlining and comments gave me an understanding of what Auntie Léa believed about the system of apartheid in South Africa, and the extent of her support for Mandela's activism. For example, in July 1988, Auntie Léa annotated two articles about Nelson Mandela published in *The Gazette*, an English-language paper published in Montreal. The first article was about Nelson Mandela's upcoming 70th birthday. The headlines read: "Anti-apartheid fighter turns 70 tomorrow – still behind bars" and "Mandela: Age hasn't dimmed his dream" (Nagle, 1988). Underneath the second headline about age not dimming Mandela's dream, Auntie Léa had written, "Bravo Nelson Mandela!" Within the article itself she had underlined and circled several paragraphs. The first underlined paragraph spoke about the crime that had led to Mandela's imprisonment in a South African prison called Pollsmoor. Pollsmoor was one of the many prisons Mandela had been incarcerated in over a period of 25 years. The paragraph read:

> His crime was treason: He counselled the use of violence and sabotage as means of ending South Africa's racial segregation and white political dominance.
>
> His cause, black liberation, has not faltered despite his age and more than a quarter century away from any public platform (Nagle, 1988, p. B1).

The last four paragraphs that were underlined and circled in the article spoke about Mandela's daughters Zindziswa and Zenani and his wife Winnie Mandela.

> Their daughters, Zindziswa and Zenani, experienced an unusual childhood – even by South African standards. At one point both parents were in prison followed by Winnie being banished from their Soweto home to Brandfort township in the Orange Free State.
>
> "My mother has made us strong," Zindzi believes. "Once in court, when mummy was convicted – I think

> it was '71 – I started crying and she said, "You must never cry, because you are giving them satisfaction if you do so.'"
>
> Winnie Mandela has turned down the government's offer of an unprecedented six-hour reunion with her husband inside Pollsmoor prison tomorrow (the day of Mandela's 70th birthday).
>
> She said she does not want to accept special privileges and wants to focus attention on other jailed opponents of apartheid (Nagle, 1988, p.B1).

Auntie Léa's annotations show us she admired the way Nelson Mandela's commitment to his cause had not wavered despite over 25 years of incarceration. She also admired Winnie Mandela and her daughters' commitment to the cause during their husband and father's years of incarceration.

The second article in *The Gazette's* 1988 coverage of Mandela's 70th birthday had the headline "South Africa clamps lid on black areas." The first two paragraphs said this:

> Hundreds of South African security forces, many in armoured vehicles, patrolled black townships outside Cape Town yesterday, bracing for Nelson Mandela's 70th birthday tomorrow.
>
> Police banned all events marking the African National Congress leader's birthday and set up road blocks around the Cape Town prison where he is confined (AP-CP, 1988, p.B1).

At the top of the article, just above the headline "South Africa clamps lid on black areas." Auntie Léa had written "Afraid of what?" and "cowards!"

Several years later, Auntie Léa saved an article from *The Gazette* that carried the headline "No longer 'skunk of the world' South Africa joins family of nations." It was also tucked inside the *For Nelson Mandela* book. The article reported on the moment that Nelson Mandela took power over South Africa's army, treasury, and courts as the first Black president in the country's history.

> "Never, never and never again shall it be that this beautiful land will again experience the oppression of one by another and suffer the indignity of being the skunk of the world," Mandela said in his inaugural address. "Let freedom reign" (Remer, 1994, p. A1).

This time, there were no annotations, no underlining, and no circles written on the article. There was no need. Nelson Mandela had said it all: "Let freedom reign."

On 10 May 1994, the day Nelson Mandela became the president of South Africa, Auntie Léa was 91 years old. She was one of the oldest activists who had marched in Montreal's anti-apartheid marches, rallies and protests. Auntie Léa believed it was important for older activists to participate in public demonstrations. "As long as I can, as long as I can talk and think," she told the Voice of Women interviewer in 1982, at the age of 79, "I will be at the protests." She continued,

> It's important that we, the elderly, participate; we can give a little sign of encouragement to the younger generation and make them think, "Goodness! If she's still fighting, how can I stay quietly at home?" (Voice of Women, 1982, p. 3).

Auntie Léa kept fighting for social causes right up until the end of her life. In the next chapter, the last chapter of her biography, I write about the ways Auntie Léa lived out the last years of her life. I also discuss the public recognition she has received for her work, and the way her legacy of activism has influenced the educators and activists who have followed her.

6
Léa Roback
Growing older (1988–2000)

> Look out the window.
> The sky's almost covered.
> Some grayish white clouds,
> Some almost black.
> But between them, you can see a bit of blue.
> I focus on the blue.
>
> – Léa Roback[32]

***

In this last chapter of Auntie Léa's biography, I discuss the thoughts Auntie Léa shared in the interviews she gave during her eighties and early nineties. I also discuss the many tributes and honours she has received for her work and reflect on the ways her activism continues to live on in the generations of educators and activists who have followed her. While much that has been written about Auntie Léa has focused on the stories she told about her activist work in the 1930s and 1940s, I found the ideas she shared towards the end of her life about growing older as an activist very compelling. Auntie Léa's ideas about love, family support and being grateful for beauty in the world while struggling against its ugliness offer today's activists helpful ways of thinking about their own activist work.

Thoughts on love

In several of the interviews Auntie Léa gave in the later years of her life, she was asked if she regretted not getting married and if growing older as a single woman with modest financial means was challenging. For example, in her interview with Auntie Léa at the age of 93, Ghila Bénesty-Sroka asked Auntie Léa if she thought she had placed her political commitments above love. In response, Auntie Léa explained:

> Love is very broad, you know. It all depends on what one wants to put into that word, the expectations one has. I was very busy; I had all kinds of things on my mind. I liked making love, it was very good. And then, a man's caress, of course, is wonderful, you can't do without it. But a husband, no (Bénesty-Sroka, 1996, p. 84).

Auntie Léa's expansive idea of love – her understanding of love as being connected to her political commitments – was, I believe, part of what sustained her passion for activism for seven decades and why she never regretted not getting married.

The closeness Auntie Léa felt to the people she worked with, and the love she felt for them, resonates in some ways with bell hooks' writing on love. hooks was an American Black feminist writer who drew from the writings of psychologist Erich Fromm. In her book *All About Love*, hooks understands love as "the will to extend one's self for the purpose of nurturing one's own or another's spiritual growth" (hooks, 2000, p. 4). Explaining further, hooks shares Fromm's argument that, "Love is as love does. Love is an act of will. It is both an intention and an action. We do not have to love. We choose to love" (hooks, 2000, p. 4). In order for community love to thrive, hooks believed people need to embrace a variety of practices including care, recognition, respect, commitment, trust, and honest and open communication.

Throughout her life Auntie Léa extended herself to nurture other people's growth. Not so much for spiritual growth (although she often told interviewers her activism was fuelled by the Jewish religious and cultural imperative to do something in the face of injustice), but perhaps for political growth. Auntie Léa worked hard to provide the people she worked with the care, recognition and respect she knew they deserved. She supported young women making hard decisions about unwanted pregnancies, protected the seniority of unionized workers, and challenged racism in hiring decisions. The people Auntie Léa worked with trusted her because she was direct and honest when she spoke to them. She had no regrets about not marrying because she had experienced love among the people she worked with in the labour and women's movements. Her ability to embrace love within her social and political movement work not only nourished her own activism, it also sustained the lifelong activism of others, like the union stewards in the factories that Auntie Léa helped to unionize.

At the same time as she showed care and respect for the people she worked with, Auntie Léa was also very opinionated, and would express her opinions forcefully when fighting for her political values. There were people she didn't hold much compassion for – like the factory bosses and people interested in profiteering – and, as discussed in Chapter 4, she would often confront them harshly when fighting for the rights of their workers. Although confrontation and intimidation often allowed Auntie Léa to meet her political goals, they also sometimes prevented her from doing the work she wanted to do. For example, after being fired from RCA, she would have liked to have worked in the Jewish social service sector but was considered too radical and unrelenting. She wasn't a person who sought consensus, a skill valued in social work within the mainstream Jewish community.

Thoughts on family support

Answering a similar question about growing older with modest financial means from Nicole Lacelle, Auntie Léa said:

> …. It never bothered me at all. I have to say that my family has always supported me. My mother always told me that the door would always be open, that there would always be a bed to sleep in and a plate on the table. It's an inner security when you have moral support … Like I said, I must not be normal, but I never thought that, once I was old, the sky would fall on my head. I told a friend who was worried: "We'll think about it when we get there."
>
> Well, now I'm there, and my goodness, I don't think about it much more. I don't have money, I can't afford to travel, but it's not a big deal. If missing something made me unhappy, that would be a different story! … I've never felt insecure. Once, I had two or three dollars left, I didn't have a job, and I spent them to go to the theatre!

> There's nothing worse than being unhappy every day (Lacelle and Roback, 2005, p. 164).

When Auntie Léa would come home after a late night union meeting, she'd always find a plate on the kitchen table prepared by her mother Fanny with something "good to nibble on" and a little note saying, "I hope you are not too tired." When she had to travel outside of Montreal, Fanny would send Auntie Léa a letter every week, and call her intercity, to ask, "What do you need? Do you want me to send you something?" (*The life of a union activist: Rose Pesotta and Léa Roback*, 2023). These were the days when long distance calls were expensive and were only made on Sunday evenings, after 8:00 p.m. when the rates were cheaper.

Additional family support came from Auntie Léa's sister Annie (the sister who hosted us for lunch before the Quebec City premiere of Sophie Bissonnette's film *Des lumières dans la grande noirceur*). Auntie Annie often sent Auntie Léa clothes she was no longer wearing. Auntie Léa, who loved beautiful dresses, blouses and jackets, embraced the second-hand clothing from Auntie Annie and her other sisters, telling Nicole Lacelle, "I've always been well-dressed with my sisters' clothes; it was an honor because they had good taste!" (Lacelle and Roback, 2005, p. 163).

In her later years, Auntie Léa's nephew – Edgar Goldstein – my dad, who was an oncology pharmacist at the Montreal Jewish Hospital, made sure that Auntie Léa was well taken care of. He and his wife Louise visited Auntie Léa regularly, helped her move from her apartment to a small seniors' residence when she no longer wanted to cook meals for herself, and made sure she had the everyday things she needed, like new underwear, stockings, and shoes. Although I was living in Toronto working on my doctorate degree by the time Auntie Léa moved into the residence, I visited often. During my visits, I could see she was still living an active, engaged life.

At the seniors' residence, Auntie Léa, who by then was in her mid-nineties, had a rigorous routine. She got up early, showered, and dressed before breakfast which she took in the dining room with the other residents. Then she went for her first walk of the day. The residence was located on a steep hill, and walking up the street kept her fit. When she returned from her walk, she'd read two daily newspapers – one French, one English. On warm days, she was able to sit outside on the small balcony to read until she was called for lunch.

After lunch, Auntie Léa would retrieve her cane and go walking again. The cane she used was first used by her grandfather, and then by her mother. It had passed through three generations of Robacks. By the time Auntie Léa got back from her second walk of the day, it was time for supper, and then after supper, in the summer, she'd take one more walk. In the winter, when it was too dark to walk after supper, Auntie Léa would go into her room and listen to the news. Auntie Léa was never a fan of television. She always called it "the idiot box." But if my dad phoned her to tell her that there was something interesting to watch on television, she might watch it.

Right up to the time she died, Auntie Léa loved music, theatre and reading. The cultural activities that sustained her passion for life and activism in her younger years, continued to sustain her passion for life as she aged. In addition to reading two daily newspapers, she also read biographies, poetry, and the occasional novel (a copy of Marge Piercy's *City of Light,* a novel about the French Revolution which I had brought as a gift was on her night table the last time we visited). Sharing her love of reading with journalist Susan Schwartz, Auntie Léa stated, "The moment you stop using your brain, you stop living" (Schwartz and Roback, 1996/1997, p. 9).

Auntie Léa also remained as political and feisty as ever. Sophie Bissonnette remembers a story about a telephone call my father Edgar received from her seniors' residence telling him that Auntie Léa was trying to unionize their staff. They wanted her to stop. When I asked my dad's wife Louise if she remembered the phone call from the residence, she said she did. She also remembered my dad talking to Auntie Léa about not antagonizing the people who managed the residence if she wanted to keep living there.

Seeing beauty in the world

In celebration of one of Auntie Léa's birthdays in her 90s, my father and Louise hosted a tea party for Auntie Léa and family who were visiting or living in Montreal. Journalist Susan Schwartz, who was writing a profile of Auntie Léa for the magazine *This Country Canada* in 1996, was invited to the party and was treated to good music, good food, and a beautiful view. She wrote:

> After spirited piano performances by [my cousin Barbara's] twins [Joshua and Noah] and a hearty toast by Edgar to Léa's continued good health, the family repaired to a dining-room table, groaning with delicacies. Léa tucked in and ate with pleasure. After a time, she stared out of the dining-room window of the eleventh-floor

apartment at the spectacular view of Montreal's skyline and the St. Lawrence River to the south. "I've been here at night, and you see right across the river. It's so beautiful. We're lucky that we still have eyes that can see and appreciate this beauty. "*C'est pas possible.*"

"*C'est pas possible*" was something Auntie Léa would often say, meaning "How is it possible that there is so much beauty in this world?" Choosing to see beauty in a world that was often ugly, was one way Auntie Léa embraced optimism in both her younger and older years. As the opening quote of this chapter shows, on a day when the sky above her was covered with dark clouds, "some almost black," Auntie Léa looked for a spot of blue. "I focus on the blue," she told Nicole Lacelle.

Tributes, honours, and legacies

When she died at the age of 96 in the summer of 2000, Auntie Léa left behind a rich legacy of activism and care that made the world a better place. That legacy has been recognized and honoured in a variety of ways. The first public recognition came in 1985, when Auntie Léa was 82 years old and became an honorary member of the Canadian Research Institute for the Advancement of Women (CRIAW). The CRIAW wanted to recognize Auntie Léa for her social and political activism around human rights, workers' rights, and women's rights.

In 1993, in honour of Auntie Léa's 90th birthday, feminist activists in Montreal established the Léa Roback Foundation, whose goal was to raise scholarship funds for socially committed and economically disadvantaged women. This honour was particularly important to Auntie Léa as it provided women without financial support the means to continue their education. She would often say, "Education is the hallmark of self-realization, and above all, a key to people's freedom!" (Léa Roback Foundation, 2015).

To celebrate the launch of the Léa Roback Foundation and Auntie Léa's 90th birthday, a brunch was arranged at La Maison Egg Roll, a restaurant in the working-class neighbourhood of St. Henri in Montreal. One hundred people attended, including peace activists, labour organizers, environmentalists, feminists, teachers, students, writers, filmmakers, family, and friends (Léa Roback Foundation, 2015; Schwartz and Roback, 1996/1997). An activist singing group called the Raging Grannies was invited to perform at the party, and a number of friends and colleagues brought prepared words of appreciation for Auntie Léa's seven decades of activism and care. Raging Granny, Mildred Ryerson, who worked with Auntie Léa in the campaign for peace, told guests, "Léa represents our dreams." Dorothy Goldin Rosenberg who was also a member of Voice of Women praised Auntie Léa as someone who had always been in the vanguard of social causes. And in the book of tributes that had been prepared for the celebration, guest Marie Mottashed wrote, "According to Jewish folklore, each generation is blessed with 36 compassionate individuals whose presence accounts for whatever goodness and justice there is in the world. I have no idea who the other 35 are, but I am certain that we have one of these select 36 in our midst" (Schwartz and Roback, 1996/1997).

Three members of my family have volunteered as members of the board which directs the Léa Roback Foundation in its work. One was Donna Mergler, whose maternal grandmother was Moishe's sister, Lottie Roback Helfield. The second was Louise Goldstein and the third is my cousin Melanie Leavitt, who has just recently replaced Louise. The first scholarship was given out in 1994 to Linda Bherer, a nurse who used the funding to complete her degree in midwifery.

Twenty years later, Leavitt reported that in 2024 the Foundation had granted 34 scholarships totalling $85,000 to recipients from age 18 to age 67. Their educational pursuits included literacy courses, French courses for recent immigrants, high school completion courses, community college diplomas and university degrees. Each of the women who received scholarships to continue their education is using what they learned to better the lives of people in their communities. They are continuing the social justice work Auntie Léa engaged in. Auntie Léa would be absolutely thrilled.

The board members of the Léa Roback Foundation are strong fundraisers, and the amount of scholarship money they have to give out each year continues to grow. For example, in 2012, the Foundation organized a benefit concert that featured songs of struggle from Paul Robeson (1898–1976). Robeson was a popular Black American singer, famous for his Negro spirituals and folk songs, who was involved in the anti-fascist, workers' rights, and civil rights movements in the first part of the twentieth century. Robeson toured through Europe and North America, played Othello on Broadway and sang *Ol' Man River* in the film *Showboat*. Robeson's activism made him a target of the House Un-American Activities Committee (HUAC) under the anti-communist politician Joseph McCarthy. Denounced as a traitor and a communist, his career was destroyed. Although he had been internationally acclaimed, he was blacklisted from performing on stage, screen, radio, and television in the United States. In 1950, the American government revoked his passport. However, after years of protest campaigns and legal action, the American Supreme Court returned his passport, and Robeson made one last concert tour. After three years of touring, he returned to the United States and retired from public life in 1963 due to ill health. He died 13 years later, at the age of 78.

The Foundation's fundraising concert that featured Paul Robeson's music reminded me of the people's and workers' concerts that Auntie Léa attended in both Berlin and Montreal when she was a member of the communist movement. Twelve years after losing Auntie Léa, the board was able to resurrect the warmth, generosity, songs, and exhilaration of comradeship that Merrily Weisbord writes about in her book *The Strangest Dream* to raise money for scholarships to be given out in her name.

The legacy of Auntie Léa's activist work also lives on in Le Centre Léa Roback, a research centre in Montreal that focuses on research into social inequalities. It also lives on in Maison Parent-Roback, a hub for community groups defending women's rights, which was established in 1997 to honour both Auntie Léa and her long-time friend and fellow activist Madeleine Parent. Maison Parent-Roback is owned and operated by ten women's organizations. It opened on 27 September 1998, with funding from a variety of foundations. Like the scholarship recipients, each of these organizations works hard to support the communities they serve.

In 1999, on National Seniors' Day, which takes place annually on the first of October, Auntie Léa's work in Quebec was recognized by the Elders Council. The following year, in April 2000, the YWCA honoured Auntie Léa at its Women of Distinction gala, once again alongside Madeleine Parent. Then, in May 2000, just a few months before she died, the Quebec government inducted Auntie Léa as a Knight of the National Order of Quebec. I attended the ceremony where Auntie Léa was given a certificate, a ribbon, and a medallion – posthumously – for her outstanding achievements. I framed the certificate, and it now hangs on a wall in my office at the University of Toronto, where I talk to my students about Auntie Léa's life and work.

I passed on the ribbon and the medallion to my cousin Lea Goldstein, who was named after Auntie Léa, on the occasion of her bat mitzvah. Lea is my Auntie Léa's great-great-niece and the great-granddaughter of my grandmother Rose. Lea's bat mitzvah took place on Zoom during the Covid lock-down. During the reading of her Torah portion, Lea sat behind a table with a tablecloth that held her reading and Auntie Léa's ribbon and medallion. It was a moment full of meaning for Lea and her family: on the day she became a young woman responsible for deciding how she would like to practice Judaism, Lea chose to remind herself of her great-great-aunt Léa's legacy of working towards social justice. Of course, Lea will find her own ways to work toward social justice in the different communities she is part of, and they may be different from the causes her great-great-auntie Léa adopted. But like so many others, I know that Lea will be inspired by her aunt's incredible courage, persistence, and optimism, as she finds her own way to make the world a better place.

In addition to having been named a Knight of the National Order of Quebec, Auntie Léa has had a street named after her in her childhood home of Beauport, a park named after her in the city of Côte Saint-Luc on the island of Montreal, and another street named after her in the Montreal neighbourhood of Saint-Henri.

Rue Léa Roback (Léa Roback Street) in Saint-Henri is not far from where the original RCA plant was located in the 1940s. Most recently, in August 2023, Canada Post released a stamp celebrating Auntie Léa alongside two other stamps honouring Quebec feminists: Madeleine Parent and Simone Monet-Chartrand.

While I was unable to attend the ceremony in Montreal that celebrated the release of the stamp, I video-recorded a message to be played at the gathering and received a full report of the event from my cousin Melanie Leavitt who was there. It was after hearing Melanie's description of the joy and excitement that accompanied the way Auntie Léa and her fellow activists Madeleine Parent and Simone Monet-Chartrand were being honoured that I began thinking about writing this story of Auntie Léa's life and activism. In closing my biography, I'd like to share one of my strongest memories of spending time with Auntie Léa.

In 1973, when I was fourteen, Auntie Léa took me to a summer theatre festival located in Stratford, Ontario. I was supposed to go to the Stratford Festival with my grandmother Rose, but she died unexpectedly in March, just before my brother Richard's bar mitzvah. My grandmother was adored by everyone in the family – as well as by everyone who knew her – and we were all devastated.

Auntie Léa knew that it was my grandmother Rose who had introduced me to live theatre. Rose took me to see a French puppet show with her when I was about five or six. The show was sold out, and my grandmother had to put our names on a waiting list. When she went to speak to the box office clerk, she spoke in French. Like Auntie Léa my grandmother was completely fluent in French, English and Yiddish and could cross language borders easily. My grandmother told the box office clerk that our last name was Gauthier (not Goldstein). When I asked her why, she said that we were more likely to get to the top of the waiting list with a French-Canadian name like Gauthier than with an English, Jewish name like Goldstein. I don't know if she was right or not, but we did get two last-minute seats under the name Gauthier. The experiences of the Roback family with anti-semitism in Beauport and Montreal in the first decades of the twentieth century encouraged my grandmother to use her skill as a fluent speaker of French to border cross between her own English Jewish community and the French-Canadian theatre community.

Like Auntie Léa, my grandmother Rose also worked for His Majesty's Theatre. It was Auntie Léa who got her a job there. Rose also sold tickets to performances put on by the Montreal Children's Theatre (MCT), a children's theatre company founded in 1933 by Dorothy Davis and Violet Waters. She reserved tickets for my brothers and me, and we attended many MCT performances. Then when I was seven or eight, my grandmother enrolled me in drama classes at MCT so I could audition for roles in the school's annual production. During the time I took classes at MCT I played the roles of a villager in *The Pied Piper* and a fairy in Cinderella.

After my grandmother's sudden death, Auntie Léa volunteered to take me to Stratford so I wouldn't miss seeing the plays my grandmother had planned for us to see. Travelling from Montreal to Stratford, Ontario with Auntie Léa involved a train ride from Montreal to Toronto, an overnight stay in Toronto, a second train ride from Toronto to Stratford, booking a room in someone's home as bed and breakfast guests, and then walking to each of the three theatres where the plays were held. Auntie Léa and I did it all. We saw three plays: Shakespeare's *The Taming of the Shrew* (a play about sexism), *Othello* (a play about racism – the same play that Paul Robeson starred in on Broadway), and a Canadian play by Henry Beissel called *Inook and the Sun*, which actually had its premiere at the 1973 Stratford Festival we attended.

Despite the wonderful theatre we saw during our trip to Stratford, my clearest memories from the trip are not about the plays we saw but all of the other things we did together. I remember going to the health food store to get lunch for our picnics in the park (it was the first time I had ever shopped in a health food store). I also remember attending a folk music concert at a club called The Black Swan (it was my first time going to a club to hear music late at night). And I remember eating breakfast at the Woolworth's lunch counter and Auntie Léa ordering breakfast in French. The teenage server, who lived in English-speaking Stratford, did not understand a word Auntie Léa said. Auntie Léa told the server, a little harshly, that because she lived in a bilingual country, she needed to learn to speak French. The server who had never been told anything like that before, and who was likely a little intimidated by Auntie Léa, nodded silently. I remember being grateful that my parents had enrolled me in a French immersion program when I was in the seventh grade and that I was currently taking forty percent of my courses in high school in French. Unlike the English-speaking server at Woolworth's in Stratford, I could read, write, and speak French even though I was a student in an English-speaking school in Montreal.

My trip to Stratford with Auntie Léa was not only a trip full of theatre, but a trip full of health food, folk music, and politics. At fourteen, I was introduced to ways of travelling and being in the world that were different from anything I'd ever experienced before. Culture – all kinds of culture, from Shakespeare to 1970s folk music, to Inuit fables – brought joy and pleasure. The kind of joy and pleasure that sustained Auntie Léa and her comrades in difficult times as activists.

A few years later, when I was in my twenties, I followed Auntie Léa and my grandmother Rose into theatre box office work. I was a university student at Concordia University studying English Literature and Women's Studies (which had not yet been renamed Women and Gender Studies) and worked part-time selling tickets at the English-language Centaur Theatre in Montreal. In the summer, I worked at an English-speaking Canadian summer theatre festival held at Bishop's University in Lennoxville, Quebec, a two-hour drive from Montreal. Many years later, after establishing a career as a researcher and teacher at the University of Toronto, I completed a master's degree in playwriting at Spalding University in Louisville, Kentucky. In 2007, at the age of 50, I founded an independent activist theatre company called Gailey Road Productions.[33] Based in Toronto, Gailey Road is a place where "research meets theatre and theatre meets research." I write research-based and verbatim theatre plays that when read aloud or performed, provide opportunities for conversations around discrimination, human rights, and activism. For example, my most recent project, *The Love Booth and Six Companion Plays*, is a set of seven short plays about histories of queer and trans activism and care in the early Lesbian, Gay, Bisexual, and Transgender (LGBT) Liberation movement (Goldstein, 2023).[34]

For readers who haven't heard the term before, a verbatim play is created by researching what people have to say about their everyday lives or about an event that has happened in their community (Brown and Wake, 2010; Goldstein, 2023). The words of these people (for example, the words of the activists I researched) are then edited, arranged, and/or recontextualized to form a dramatic monologue or play script, which can be performed on stage by actors who take on the characters of the real individuals whose words are being used (Hammond and Stewart, 2008).

The first play in my project, *The Love Booth*, tells the story of lesbian activists Barbara Gittings and Kay Lahusen who became partners in life and a created a family of choice that supported their activism in the early 1970s to delist homosexuality from the American Psychiatric Association (APA)'s *Diagnostic and Statistical Manual of Mental Disorders* (DSM). The six companion plays tell the stories of other moments of activism and other families of choice created by queer and trans activists and their allies. They include stories of activism undertaken by gay men to support the presidential campaign of Shirley Chisholm, the first Black woman to run for President in the United States in 1973; the activist work done by Iris de la Cruz to challenge the stigma and shame of living with HIV in the 1980s; the creation of Kitchen Table –Women of Colour Press by Black lesbian poet Audre Lorde and Black scholar and writer Barbara Smith; the poetry writing of Two-Spirit artist and activist Chrystos which was published in Cherríe Moraga and Gloria Anzaldúa's groundbreaking 1981 book *This Bridge Called My Back*; and the activism of trans activists Marsha P. Johnson, Sylvia Rivera, and Chelsea Goodwin to provide shelter for homeless young drag queens, gay youth, and trans women living in New York. Gailey Road staged a production of *The Love Booth and Six Companion Plays* for the Toronto Pride Festival in 2023. The performance provided me, the director, the cast, and the audience with the same kind of joy and pleasure Auntie Léa had received from the theatre performances she attended.[35]

I first began thinking about writing a biography about Auntie Léa's life and activism after the stamp created in her honour was released in the summer of 2023. I began conducting archival research at the Jewish Public Library in Montreal in January 2024, and began writing in May 2024, in preparation for attending my first Biography International Conference. I thought I would get more out of the conference if I started to write the biography before the conference began. The conference was held in New York City, and I was able to get a ticket to the Broadway musical *Suffs*, a play about the American suffrage movement by theatre artist Shaina Taub. Knowing that I would be researching Auntie Léa's participation in the Quebec suffrage movement, I thought it would be inspirational to see and hear how Taub staged moments of the suffragists' activism on stage.

The show was sold out the night I saw it. We were an enthusiastic audience. The theatre was filled with young people, many of them young women, some of whom had come with their mothers and grandmothers. In May 2024, Americans were preparing to vote in a national election, and the audience was eager to hear stories about the nineteenth- and twentieth-century activists who fought for women to have the right to vote. At the end of the play, the entire cast came out to sing a song that sounded like a call to activism from the suffragists on stage to the people in the audience. The song was called "Keep Marching" and the chorus went like this:

> Cause your ancestors are all the proof you need
> That progress is possible, not guaranteed
> It will only be made only if we
> Keep marching, keep marching on …
> … Yes, the world can be changed
> We've done it before
> So keep marching, keep marching
>   (Taub, 2024).

The idea that progress is possible, but not guaranteed is an idea that Auntie Léa knew to be true. What Auntie Léa also knew to be true was that the only way progress could be made is by marching and protesting against discrimination and inequality. Auntie Léa spent her life marching and protesting. She provided proof to her nephews and nieces and all of the young people who followed her that the world could be changed – but only if they kept marching. I hope this biography of Léa Roback's activist life of community love and care inspires you to keep marching, in whatever way you think is needed. And when times get tough, I also hope it inspires you to focus on the blue.

Notes

1. Katz, H. (1993). "Knitting Isn't My Passion – Social Causes Are." *The Gazette*, 2 Dec. 1993, p. 5.

2. Like many people who use the terms great-niece or great-nephew interchangeably, I have always referred to Auntie Léa as my great-aunt, and myself as her great-niece. However, Ancestry.com tells us that "grand" means two generations apart, "great" means three generations apart, and "great-great" means four generations apart. So according to Ancestry.com, Auntie Léa is my grand-aunt, and I am her grand-niece.

3. Fascism can be defined as a set of far-right, authoritarian, ultranationalist political ideas and beliefs. It is opposed to other political ideologies (political ideas and beliefs) such as democracy, pluralism, egalitarianism, liberalism, socialism, and Marxism.

4. More information about the global, survivor-run MeToo movement can be found at: https://metoomvmt.org/

5. For an example of this research and the way I have shared my archival research in the form of a verbatim playscript please see *The Love Booth and Six Companion Plays* (Goldstein, 2023), which is a set of seven short verbatim plays about queer and trans activism in the United States between the 1940s and the1980s. To read the script and hear the plays on the Gailey Road website, go to: https://gaileyroad.com/the-love-booth-companion-plays/.

6. To view the film with English subtitles, visit the Cinémathèque Québécoise website at: https://www.cinematheque.qc.ca/en/dossiers/sophie-bissonnette/des-lumieres-dans-la-grande-noirceur/.

7. A bar mitzvah is a Jewish ceremony held to celebrate a boy reaching the age of 13. A bat mitzvah celebrates a girl turning 12. After their bar mitzvah or bat mitzvah, young people are responsible for their own actions and can decide for themselves how they would like to practice Judaism. Recently, to celebrate transgender and nonbinary young people, some synagogues and Jewish communities have adopted "they mitzvahs", "b'nai mitzvahs", or "b mitzvahs".

8. Cisheternormative activist histories are histories that centre the activism of cisgender and heterosexual people. Cisgender people are those whose gender identity corresponds with the sex registered for them at birth. Transgender people are those whose gender identity does not correspond with the sex registered for them at birth. The "plus" in LGBTQIA2S+ signifies additional identity terms not already included in the acronym.

9. Bénesty-Sroka, G. (1996). Entrevue avec Léa Roback: Une femme engagée. *Canadian Woman Studies/Les cahiers de la femme,* 16(4), p. 81.

10. The Torah is made up of the first five books of the Hebrew Bible: Genesis, Exodus, Leviticus, Numbers, and Deuteronomy. The Talmud describes and explains Jewish religious laws and Jewish theology.

11. Moishe and Harry walked eight and a half kilometres to their synagogue in Quebec City on Saturdays because religious Jews don't drive on the Sabbath, the Jewish day of rest.

12. To read more about Canada's refusal to admit European Jewish refugees into the country between 1933 and 1948, please see the 40th anniversary edition of *None Is Too Many* by Irving Abella and Harold Troper published in 2023.

13. To read more about the political work of Jewish Voice for Peace, see: https://www.jewishvoiceforpeace.org/. For recommended readings on the conflict, please see the section called "Further Reading" at the end of the biography.

14. The patterned black and white *keffiyeh* is a symbol of Palestinian nationalism and resistance and dates back to the 1936–1939 revolt in Palestine.
15. *Des lumières dans la grande noirceur*, 1991.
16. Communism is a sociopolitical, philosophical, and economic ideology (a set of ideas and beliefs) as well as an economic system (a way of creating and sharing wealth). In a communist system, individual people do not own land, factories, or machinery (the means of production). Instead, the government or the whole community owns the means of production.
17. German artist Käthe Kollwitz (1867–1945) was known for her etching and sculpture work, and later for lithography and woodcuts. Her work centred on women, the working class, and people in need (Mahler, 2016).
18. I have written about *Kristallnacht* in my novel *Home of Her Heart*, which was published by Gailey Road Productions in 2023. An audio recording of the novel is available on the Gailey Road website at: https://gaileyroad.com/publicati ons-2018-2027/
19. Before the Hidden Book Shop and Modern Bookshop opened, Hirsch Hershman, a Jewish immigrant from Romania who worked in a women's clothing shop, opened a Jewish bookstore in 1902. It was intended to make socialist newspapers, published in Yiddish in New York, available to readers in Montreal. The bookstore also sold Yiddish translations of books by Russian writer Leo Tolstoy and French writers Émile Zola and Paul Lafargue. The bookstore became a gathering place for Jewish immigrant intellectuals in Montreal (Anctil and Woodsworth, 2021, p.84).
20. Bénesty-Sroka, G. (1996). Entrevue avec Léa Roback: Une femme engagée. *Canadian Woman Studies/Les cahiers de la femme,* 16(4), p. 82.
21. Calamity Jane (Martha Jane Burke) was an American who lived in the second half of the 19th century and was famous

for her skill at riding horses and shooting guns. She dressed in men's clothing and was known for saying that she would bring calamity and harm to anyone who made her angry.

22. French Canadian writer Gabrielle Roy's (1909–1983) novel *Bonheur d'occasion*, published in 1945, portrayed the lives of families living in St. Henri between the 1940s and 1960s. The novel was published in 1947 in English as *The Tin Flute*.

23. The language which Auntie Léa was speaking to the security guard was French. In French, there are two ways to address someone – formally with respect by using *vous* and informally with familiarity by using *tu*. The security guard addressed Auntie Léa informally with familiarity even though she had addressed him formally with respect. Her demand that the security guard address her using *vous* was a demand for respect.

24. *An Activist in Search of Employment (1950s and 1960s)*, 2023.

25. The histories of how the First Nations and Inuit Peoples, and Asian Canadians challenged settler colonialism and racism and fought for the right to vote in Canada are explained in further detail in the following websites:

    First Nations Peoples

    https://electionsanddemocracy.ca/voting-rights-through-time-0/first-nations-and-right-vote-case-study

    Inuit Peoples

    https://electionsanddemocracy.ca/voting-rights-through-time-0/inuit-and-right-vote-case-study

    Asian Canadianshttps://electionsanddemocracy.ca/voting-rights-through-time-0/brief-history-federal-voting-rights-canada

26. Idola Saint-Jean founded the Alliance, and after Thérèse Casgrain, is considered the second most important figure in the history of Quebec's suffrage movement. Carrie Derrick and Anna Marks Lyman also worked with these groups,

and Carrie Derrick was the founder of the Montreal Suffrage Association.

27. After women won the right to vote and run for office, both Casgrain and Saint-Jean ran as candidates at the federal level. Saint-Jean ran as an independent Liberal in the riding of Saint-Denis in 1930, becoming the first French-speaking woman in Québec to run as a candidate. She came in third. Casgrain stood for election in 1942 also as an independent Liberal. While Casgrain was defeated nine times in provincial and federal elections between 1942 and 1962, she did become the first woman to lead a Québec political party. In 1951, Casgrain was elected to head the provincial wing of the Co-operative Commonwealth Federation (CCF), which is now the New Democratic Party (NDP) in Canada. See Chapter 3 for another story about the NDP.

28. Women who participated in the suffrage movement in Canada were known as both "suffragists", those who campaigned using peaceful methods such as lobbying, and "suffragettes", those who believed in more militant strategies to win the right to vote. The women who were part of the *Ligue des droits de la femme* were generally known as suffragists, not suffragettes, even though Casgrain uses the word "suffragettes" here.

29. Readers can listen to the protest song at: https://www.youtube.com/watch?v=8yHRPX7WIS8

30. Abortion access widely varies across Canada. – Joan Bryden. *The Ottawa Citizen*. 30 Jan. 1988. pg. B.6

31. By the time the Court ruled on Daigle's case, Daigle had already had a late second-term abortion in the United States. While the case had been fast-tracked, the progress was so slow that Daigle would have been in the third trimester had she waited for the ruling to be handed down.

32. Lacelle and Roback, 2005, p.173.

33. To learn more about Gailey Road Productions, please see https://gaileyroad.com/

34. The acronym LGBT (Lesbian, Gay, Bisexual, Trans) is used here instead of the contemporary acronym LGBTQ+ (Lesbian, Gay, Bisexual, Trans, Queer, Plus) because it was the acronym used at the time.

35. A copy of the script and an audio-recording of the play we recorded are both available on the Gailey Road website.

Discussion questions

1. What moments in Léa Roback's childhood and family life were key to the development of her desire to become an activist? What moments in Léa Roback's travels to Berlin were influential in the development of her political understanding of the world?
2. Léa Roback used her life experiences as a Jewish, working-class, trilingual woman to cross borders in her activist work. How do you use your own varied life experiences to cross borders in your own work?
3. Activists often have to work within or alongside institutional beliefs and practices that need to be confronted, negotiated, and addressed in order to move forward. For example, Léa Roback needed to challenge the beliefs and practices of the Catholic Church in Québec and challenge some of the beliefs and practices of the International Ladies' Garment Workers' Union. How did Roback take up these challenges?
4. Léa Roback used her position as Education Director in the International Ladies' Garment Workers' Union to begin unionizing work. How might educators use their positions and work to support social justice movements and causes?
5. This biography of Léa Roback's life and activism included a variety of excerpts from the interviews she gave to Nicole

Lacelle, Sophie Bissonnette, and others. Many people have found Roback's thoughts and words to be inspirational. Were there any thoughts or words that you found to be inspirational? What were they, and in what ways did they inspire you?

References

A Jewish Seniors' Residence Founded by Her Grandmother (1910s or 1920s) (2023). [video] Directed by S. Bissonnette. Montreal: Sophie Bissonnette. Available at: https://www.cinematheque.qc.ca/en/dossiers/pionnieres-du-feminisme-et-du-syndicalisme/lea-roback/ [Accessed 28 Aug. 2024].

An Activist in Search of Employment (1950s and 1960s) (2023). [video] Directed by S. Bissonnette. Montreal: Sophie Bissonnette. Available at: https://www.cinematheque.qc.ca/en/dossiers/pionnieres-du-feminisme-et-du-syndicalisme/lea-roback/ [Accessed 27 Jun. 2024].

Anctil, P. and Woodsworth, J. (2021). *History of the Jews in Quebec*. Ottawa, Ontario: University of Ottawa Press.

Anzaldúa, G. (2018). *Borderlands/La Frontera: The New Mestiza*. San Francisco: Aunt Lute Books.

AP-CP (1988). South Africa clamps lid on black areas. *The Gazette*, 17 Jul., p. B1.

Bénesty-Sroka, G. (1996). Entrevue avec Léa Roback: Une femme engagée. *Canadian Woman Studies/Les cahiers de la femme*, 16(4), pp. 81–85. Available at: https://cws.journals.yorku.ca/index.php/cws/article/view/9184/8301/ [Accessed 19 Jul. 2024].

Boyko, J. (2021). Bomarc Missile Crisis. [online] The Canadian Encyclopedia. Available at: https://www.thecanadianencyclopedia.ca/en/article/bomarc-missile-crisis.

Brown, P. and Wake, C. (2010). Towards a working definition of verbatim theatre. In P. Brown, ed., *Verbatim: Staging Memory and Community*. Currency Press. pp. 2–5.

Casgrain, T.F. (1972). *A Woman in a Man's World*. Toronto: McClelland and Stewart.

Clearly, A. and Clearly M. (1959). *Strontium 90*. [audio recording] Panco Records.

Cutler, S. (2017). The Midinette Spring. *Briarpatch Magazine*. 30 Jun. Available at: https://briarpatchmagazine.com/articles/view/the-midinette-spring/ [Accessed 9 Jul. 2024].

Des lumières dans la grande noirceur/A Vision in the Darkness (1991). [video] Directed by S. Bissonnette. Montreal: Les Productions Contre-jour Inc. Available at: https://www.cinematheque.qc.ca/fr/dossiers/sophie-bissonnette/des-lumieres-dans-la-grande-noirceur/ [Accessed 22 Jul. 2024].

Dworkin, A. (1981). *Pornography: Men Possessing Women*. Women's Press.

Dworkin, A. and MacKinnon, C.A. (1988). *Pornography and Civil Rights: A New Day for Women's Equality*. Minneapolis: Organizing Against Pornography.

Fink, M. (2021). *Forget Burial: HIV Kinship, Disability, and Queer/Trans Narratives*. Rutgers University Press.

Fuller, J. and Blackley, S. (2000). *Restricted Entry: Censorship on Trial*. 2nd ed. Vancouver: Press Gang Publishers.

Gidlow, E. (1986). *I Come With My Songs: The Autobiography of Elsa Gidlow*. San Francisco: Bootlegger Press.

Goldstein, T. (2023). *The Love Booth and Six Companion Plays*. With contributions from Alec Butler and Jenny Salisbury. Gailey Road Productions. Available at: https://gaileyroad.com/the-love-booth-other-plays/ [Accessed 7 Sep. 2024].

Hammond, W. and Stewart, D. (2008). *Verbatim Verbatim: Contemporary Documentary Theatre*. London: Oberon Books.

Harris, E. and Roback, L. (1988). *Interview with Léa Roback.* [sound recording]. 17 Mar. Available at: https://www.cjhn.ca/link/cjhn50059/ [Accessed 31 Jul. 2024].

Herd, A. (2006). Canada and the Cold War. [online] The Canadian Encyclopedia. Available at: https://www.thecanadianencyclopedia.ca/en/article/cold-war.

Homeboys Productions Ltd. (2018). *Little Sister's vs. Big Brother.* [video] City of Vancouver Archives, AM1675-S5-2018-020.3100. Available at: https://searcharchives.vancouver.ca/little-sisters-vs-big-brother [Accessed 10 Nov. 2024].

hooks, b. (2000). *All About Love: New Visions.* New York City: William Morrow.

Jensen, R. (2010). Pornography and the Military. *CounterPunch.* 18 Jun. Available at: https://www.counterpunch.org/2010/06/18/pornography-and-the-military/.

Jewish Public Library (2024a). *Episode 1: Upon Arrival.* [podcast]. recollections with the Jewish Public Library. Available at: https://jpl-curates.org/recollections [Accessed 1 Jun. 2024].

Jewish Public Library (2024b). *Episode 2: Hereness.* [podcast]. recollections with the Jewish Public Library. Available at: https://jpl-curates.org/recollections/ [Accessed 8 Jun. 2024].

Jewish Public Library (2024c). *Episode 3-Labour of love* [podcast]. recollections with the Jewish Public Library. Available at: https://jpl-curates.org/recollections/ [Accessed 15 Jun. 2024].

Jewish Voice for Peace (2023). On Antisemitism, Anti-Zionism and Dangerous Conflations. *Jewish Voice of Peace News.* 16 Nov. Available at: https://www.jewishvoiceforpeace.org/2023/11/09/antisemitism-dangerous/ [Accessed 27 Aug. 2024].

Jewish Voice for Peace (2024). About. [online] Available at: https://www.jewishvoiceforpeace.org/about/ [Accessed 27 Aug. 2024].

Joining the Communist Party in Berlin (1932) (2023). [video] Directed by S. Bissonnette. Montreal: Sophie Bissonnette. Available at: https://www.cinematheque.qc.ca/en/dossiers/pionnieres-du-feminisme-et-du-syndicalisme/lea-roback/ [Accessed 27, Jun. 2024].

Klein, B. S. (1981). Not a Love Story: A Film about Pornography. [video] Available at https://collection.nfb.ca/film/not_a_love_story_a_film_about_pornography [Accessed 2 Oct. 2024].

Klein, N. (2023). *Doppelganger: A Trip into the Mirror World.* Knopf Canada.

Lacelle, N. and Roback, L. (2005). *Entretiens avec Madeleine Parent et Léa Roback.* 2nd ed. Translated by ChatGPT 4.0. Montréal: Les éditions remue du ménage.

Léa Roback Foundation (2015). A historic brunch. *Bulletin d'Information.* 11 May. Available at: https://www.fondationlearoback.org/wp-content/uploads/2019/09/FLRBulletin11aweb.pdf.

Leeder, E. (1993). *The Gentle General: Rose Pesotta, Anarchist and Labor Organizer.* Albany: State University of New York Press.

Lévesque, A. and Clapperton-Richard, A. (2018). Radical Bookshops in 1930s Montréal. [online] *Remember, Resist, Redraw: A Radical History Project.* Available at: https://graphichistorycollective.com/project/poster-16-bookstores [Accessed 22 Jun. 2024].

Logan, N. (2024). How Jewish Canadians are coping with rising antisemitism after being target of bomb threats. *CBC News.* 25 Aug. Available at: https://www.cbc.ca/news/canada/canada-anti-semitism-jewish-community-1.7304013 [Accessed 27 Aug. 2024].

Long, L. (2006). Abortion in Canada [online] The Canadian Encyclopedia. Available at: https://www.thecanadianencyclopedia.ca/en/article/abortion.

Lorde, A. (2021). *Sister Outsider.* 2nd ed. Crossing Press. (Originally published 1984).

Lorde, A. (1983). There is no hierarchy of oppressions. *Bulletin: Homophobia and Education*, 14(3). Council on Interracial Books for Children.

Mahler, L. (2016). *Käthe Kollwitz*. [online] The Museum of Modern Art. Available at: https://www.moma.org/artists/3201 [Accessed 11 Oct. 2024].

Malatino, H. (2020). *Trans Care*. Minneapolis: University of Minnesota Press.

McCord Stewart Museum (2019). *Lucien Lacouture*. [online] EncycloFashionQC. Available at: https://encyclomodeqc.musee-mccord-stewart.ca/en/entry/lucien-lacouture/ [Accessed 9 Sep. 2024].

Macpherson, K. and de Bruin, T. (2020). *Canadian Voice of Women for Peace*. [online] The Canadian Encyclopedia. Available at: https://www.thecanadianencyclopedia.ca/en/article/voice-of-women [Accessed 12 Oct. 2024].

Moraga, C. and Anzaldúa, G. (2015). *This Bridge Called My Back*. State University of New York Press. (Originally published 1981).

Morgan, R. (1978). *Going Too Far: The Personal Chronicle of a Feminist*. Vintage Books.

Nagle, P. (1988). Mandela: Age hasn't dimmed his dream *The Gazette*, 17 Jul., p. B1.

Nasu, M. and Nishimura, S. (2019). *Hiroshima: A Tragedy Never to Be Repeated*. Translated by J. King and Y. Tamaka. Funuinkan Shoten Publishers.

NDP (2019). *A New Deal for People: New Democrats' Commitments to You*. [online] Canada's NDP. Available at: https://www.ndp.ca/commitments [Accessed 30 Sep. 2024].

Nelson Mandela Foundation (2024). *Biography of Nelson Mandela – Nelson Mandela Foundation*. [online] Available at: https://www.nelsonmandela.org/biography.

Owis, B. (2024). *Towards a Queer and Trans Ethic of Care in Education: Beyond the Limitations of White, Cisheteropatriarchal, Colonial Care.* London: Routledge.

Parks Canada Directory of Federal Heritage Designations (2024). *Montréal Dressmakers' Strike of 1937 National Historic Event.* [online] Available at: https://www.pc.gc.ca/apps/dfhd/page_nhs_eng.aspx?id=12098&i=76899 [Accessed 11 Oct. 2024].

PEN America (2024). *Book Bans.* [online] Available at: https://pen.org/book-bans/.

PEN Canada (2023). *Book Bans and Justice of the Imagination.* [online] Available at: https://pencanada.ca/blog/book-bans-and-justice-of-the-imagination/ [Accessed 2 Oct. 2024].

Pesotta, R. (1944). French-Canadian girls get tough. In: *Bread Upon the Waters.* New York City: Dodd, Mead and Company, pp. 262–277.

Piepzna-Samarasinha, L.L. (2018). *Care Work: Dreaming Disability Justice.* Vancouver: Arsenal Pulp Press.

Pomerleau, A. and Roback. L. (n.d.) Léa Roback: An Interview with "An Unruly Old Lady." *De la tête au coeur.* Available in the Léa Roback archives at the Jewish Public Library, Montreal, Quebec.

Poverty in the Neighbourhood of Saint-Henri (1930s and 1940s) (2023). [video] Directed by S. Bissonnette. Montreal: Sophie Bissonnette. Available at: https://www.cinematheque.qc.ca/en/dossiers/pionnieres-du-feminisme-et-du-syndicalisme/lea-roback/ [Accessed 9 Sep. 2024].

Racism in the Dressmaking Industry (1937–1939) (2023). [video] Directed by S. Bissonnette. Montreal: Sophie Bissonnette. Available at: https://www.cinematheque.qc.ca/en/dossiers/pionnieres-du-feminisme-et-du-syndicalisme/lea-roback/ [Accessed 27 Jun. 2024].

Reilly, J.N. (2006). *Winnipeg General Strike.* [online] The Canadian Encyclopedia. Available at: https://www.thecanadianencyclopedia.ca/en/article/winnipeg-general-strike [Accessed 7 Sep. 2024].

Remer, T. (1994). No longer 'skunk of the world' South African joins family of nations. *The Gazette,* 11 May, p. A1.

Reuters, T. (2024). Dutch PM 'ashamed' by Amsterdam attacks on Israeli soccer fans. *CBC News*. 9 Nov. Available at: https://www.cbc.ca/news/world/amsterdam-clashes-football-israeli-1.7377872 [Accessed 11 Nov. 2024].

Root, M.P.P. (ed.) (1996). *The Multiracial Experience: Racial Borders as a New Frontier.* Thousand Oaks: Sage Publications.

Schwartz, S. and Roback, L. (1996/1997). Lea the Lionhearted. *This Country Canada*, pp. 3–11.

Setterington, K. (2013). *Branded By the Pink Triangle.* Toronto: Second Story Press.

Strong-Boag, V. (2016). *Women's Movements in Canada: 1960–85.* [online] The Canadian Encyclopedia. Available at: https://www.thecanadianencyclopedia.ca/en/article/womens-movements-in-canada-196085 [Accessed 2 Oct. 2024].

Taub, S. (2024). Keep Marching - Suffs on Broadway. [video] YouTube. Available at: https://www.youtube.com/watch?v=XPyKqoRKT8g

The Life of a Union Activist: Rose Pesotta and Léa Roback (1930s) (2023). [video] Directed by S. Bissonnette. Montreal: Sophie Bissonnette. Available at: https://www.cinematheque.qc.ca/en/dossiers/pionnieres-du-feminisme-et-du-syndicalisme/lea-roback/ [Accessed 27 Jun. 2024].

Trujillo, C. (ed.) (1997). *Living Chicana Theory.* Thousand Oaks: Sage.

Unwanted Pregnancies: The Miséricorde Hospital and Clandestine Abortions (1930s and 1940s) (2023). [video] Directed by S. Bissonnette. Montreal: Sophie Bissonnette. Available at: https://www.cinematheque.qc.ca/en/dossiers/pionnieres-du-feminisme-et-du-syndicalisme/lea-roback/ [Accessed 27 Jun. 2024].

United States Holocaust Memorial Museum (2019). *Kristallnacht*. [online] Holocaust Encyclopedia. Available at: https://encyclopedia.ushmm.org/content/en/article/kristallnacht/ [Accessed 7 Sep. 2024].

United States Holocaust Memorial Museum (2021). *Introduction to the Holocaust*. [online] Holocaust Encyclopedia. Available at: https://encyclopedia.ushmm.org/content/en/article/introduction-to-the-holocausst/ [Accessed 7 Sep. 2024].

United States Holocaust Memorial Museum (2022a). *Hitler Comes to Power*. [online] Holocaust Encyclopedia. Available at: https://encyclopedia.ushmm.org/content/en/article/hitler-comes-to-power [Accessed 7 Sep. 2024].

United States Holocaust Memorial Museum (2022b). *Nazi Racism*. [online] Holocaust Encyclopedia. Available at: https://encyclopedia.ushmm.org/content/en/article/nazi-racism.

Uprichard, L. (2019). Montreal's Sappho. *Articulation Magazine*. 23 Oct. Available at: http://www.articulationmagazine.com/montreals-sappho/#easy-footnote-12-4515 [Accessed 30 Sep. 2024].

Voice of Women. (1982). *My Choice is Peace: An Organizing Guide for Disarmament and Development*. Voice of Women, p. 3.

Weisbord, M. (2022). *The Strangest Dream – Canadian Communists, the Spy Trials and the Cold War*. 3rd ed. Montréal: Véhicule Press.

Westley, M. (1991). *Remembrances of Grandeur: The Anglo-Protestant Elite of Montreal 1900–1950*. Editions Libre Expression.

Wikipedia (n.d.). Feminist views on pornography. [online] Available at: https://en.wikipedia.org/wiki/Feminist_views_on_pornography#:~:text=In%20its%20mission%20statement%2C%20Feminists,stifle%20efforts%20for%20social%20change [Accessed 11 May 2025].

Wise, W. (2014). *Not a Love Story: A Film about Pornography*. [online] The Canadian Encyclopedia. Available at: https://www.thecanadianencyclopedia.ca/en/article/not-a-love-story-a-film-about-pornography [Accessed 2 Oct. 2024].

Recommended further reading

Antisemitism

Abella, I. and Troper, H. (2023). *None Is Too Many: Canada and the Jews of Europe 1933–1948.* 40th anniversary edition. New Jewish Press.

Tells the story of Canada's response to the plight of European Jews during the Nazi era and its immediate aftermath, exploring why and how Canada turned its back and hardened its heart against the entry of Jewish refugees. Traces the origins and results of Canadian immigration policies towards Jews and demonstrates the ideas and practices against admitting them were pervasive and rooted in antisemitism.

Goldstein, P. (2022). *A Convenient Hatred: The History of Antisemitism.* Facing History and Ourselves.

Published by Facing History and Ourselves, a community education organization that supports public school teachers and students in understanding histories of genocide in the world in the twentieth and twenty-first centuries. Updated in 2022, the book traces antisemitism's evolution over the centuries and examines how it continues to shape attitudes and beliefs in the world today.

Khouri, R. and Wilkinson, J. (2023). *The Wall Between: What Jews and Palestinians Don't Want to Know About Each Other.* Olive Branch Press.

A book about the wall of distrust, enmity, and hate that exists between Jewish and Palestinian communities in the Diaspora and an attempt to break down the wall by examining the role propaganda and disinformation play in cementing trauma-induced fears that exist in both communities.

Lerman, A. (2022). *Whatever Happened to Antisemitism? Redefinition and the Myth of the 'Collective Jew'*. Pluto Press.

An examination of how antisemitism has been politicised over the past 30 years, and the damaging consequences of its redefinition: the suppression of free speech on Palestine/Israel, the legitimization of Islamophobic right-wing forces, and the politicization of principled opposition to antisemitism.

Canadian Communism

Weisbord, M. (2022). *The Strangest Dream – Canadian Communists, the Spy Trials and the Cold War*. 3rd ed. Montreal: Véhicule Press.

A book about Canadian communists that brings to life the history and life of militants from the 1930s to the 1956 Khrushchev revelations about Stalin.

Israel and Palestine

Khalidi, R. (2020). *The Hundred Years' War on Palestine: A History of Settler Colonial Conquest and Resistance, 1917–2017*. Macmillan.

A history of one hundred years of war against the Palestinians told through pivotal events and family history.

Khouri, R. and Wilkinson, J. (2023). *The Wall Between: What Jews and Palestinians Don't Want to Know About Each Other*. Olive Branch Press.

A book about the wall of distrust, enmity, and hate that exists between Jewish and Palestinian communities in the Diaspora and an attempt to break down the wall by examining the role propaganda and disinformation play in cementing trauma-induced fears that exist in both communities.

Jewish communities in Montréal and Québec

Anctil, P. and Woodsworth, J. (2021). *History of the Jews of Quebec*. Montreal: Boréal.

Describes the history of the Jewish community in Montreal and Quebec.

Léa Roback

Bissonnette, S. (dir.), (1991). *Des lumières dans la grande noirceur/ A Vision in the Darkness*. [video] Montreal: Les Productions Contre-jour Inc. [Accessed 22 Jul. 2024]. Available at: https://www.cinematheque.qc.ca/fr/dossiers/sophie-bissonnette/des-lumieres-dans-la-grande-noirceur/ (available with English subtitles).

A documentary film that shares the life and activism of Léa Roback during a period of Quebec history known as *La Grande Noirceur*, the Great Darkness. The film is accompanied by an English dossier with excerpts from interviews in the film available worldwide at https://www.cinematheque.qc.ca/en/dossiers/pionnieres-du-feminisme-et-du-syndicalisme/lea-roback/

Freedman, A. (2022). *Léa: A Novel*. Montreal: Linda Leith Publishing.

A novel based on the life of Léa Roback.

Lacelle, N. (2005). *Entretiens avec Madeleine Parent et Léa Roback*. Les éditions remue du ménage. (Originally published 1988).

A set of interviews with Quebec activists Léa Roback and Madeleine Parent.

Rose Pesotta

Leeder, E. (1993). *The Gentle General*. State University of New York Press.

A biography of Rose Pesotta, the organizer and vice president of the International Ladies Garment Workers' Union (ILGWU) from 1933 to 1944.

Pesotta, R. (1944). *Bread Upon the Waters*. Dodd, Mead and Company.

An autobiography that focuses on Pesotta's work as a labour organizer in the 1930s and 1940s.

Pesotta, R. (1958). *Days of Our Lives*. Excelsior Publishers.

An autobiography that tells the story of Pesotta's immigration to the United States as a Jewish immigrant from Ukraine. Includes stories about Pesotta's work as a seamstress in a shirtwaist factory and then a labour organizer.

Thérèse Casgrain

Casgrain, T. (1972). *A Woman in a Man's World*. Toronto: McClelland and Stewart.

An autobiography that reflects upon Casgrain's suffragist work, political work for the Cooperative Commonwealth Federation (CCF), which later became the New Democratic Party, and her work with the anti-nuclear peace group *La voix des femmes*/The Voice of Women. Casgrain was a politician, radio journalist and activist in the cause of human rights, prison reform, equality, and child welfare. Her contributions to Canadian political life are a testament to her belief that "if society is to be improved, a greater number of competent women must make their presence felt in all spheres of life, politics included."

The labour movement in Quebec in the 1930s and 1940s

Dion, G. (1987). *The History of the Labour Movement in Quebec*. Black Rose Books.

An examination of the development of Quebec's labour movement, focusing on the events and challenges of the 1930s and 1940s.

The women's movement in Quebec and Canada

Baillargeon, D. (2014). *A Brief History of Women in Quebec*. Wilfrid Laurier University Press.

An account of the experiences of women in Quebec from the period of European contact to the twenty-first century, discussing themes like demography, work, education, religion, and political activism.

Rebick, J. (2005). *Ten Thousand Roses: The Making of a Feminist Revolution*. Penguin Canada.

A compilation of stories from over a hundred feminists across Canada, detailing their struggles and achievements in areas such as legalized abortion, pay equity, and anti-racism efforts.

Ricci, A. (2023). *Countercurrents: Women's Movements in Postwar Montreal*. McGill-Queen's University Press.

An examination of the feminist movement in Montreal from the postwar period to the 1990s, highlighting the roles of diverse groups such as the Quebec Native Women's Association and the Congress of Black Women.

Index

Abella, Irving 152

abortion 10, 14, 96, 97, 99, 105, 112, 113, 116–120, 123, 155

activist community care 11, 13, 17

Anctil, Pierre 3, 19, 24, 28, 29, 31, 64, 70, 153

Anti-apartheid 96, 126, 127, 129

antisemitism 19, 27–32, 34–36, 51, 53, 57, 145

Anzaldúa, Gloria 12, 13, 148

Archival research 13, 14, 18, 149

Atomic bomb 109, 110

Baillargeon, Denyse 16

Beauport (Quebec) 2–5, 25–30, 33, 36, 38, 47, 51, 142, 145

Bénesty-Sroka, Ghila 20, 21, 25, 28, 30, 31, 36, 37, 50, 54, 60, 101, 132, 152, 153

Berlin 7–9, 42, 50, 51, 53–55, 58–60, 69, 108, 141, 157

Bissonnette, Sophie 8, 15–19, 23, 27, 28, 38, 41, 42, 50, 54, 68, 84, 88–91, 96, 113, 115, 135, 137, 158

Border crossing 12, 17, 47

community care 11, 13, 17

Canadian Communist Party 73

Casgrain, Thérèse 97, 99–105, 154

Catholic Church 29, 48, 66, 76, 79, 80, 85, 157

communism 7, 57, 67, 70, 85, 153

Cutler, Sophia 76, 80

Dion, Gérard 170

Dressmaker Strike, The 83–87

Duplessis, Maurice 15, 66, 84, 85, 90, 94, 103

Fascism 7, 64–65, 151

Fink, Marty 13

Freedman, Ariela 169

Gailey Road Productions 13, 147, 153, 155

gay activism 147, 148

Gidlow, Elsa 43–44

Goldstein, Edgar 135

Goldstein, Lea 135, 142

Goldstein, Rose Roback 39

Harris, Erin 30, 77

Hitler, Adolf 8, 53, 56–60, 64, 87

Hiroshima 109–111

hooks, bell 13, 132, 133

International Ladies' Garment Workers Union (ILGWU) 9, 11, 69, 74, 75, 77, 78, 85, 86, 89, 157

Jewish Voice of Peace 36, 37, 152

Kollwitz, Käthe 56, 153

Khalidi, Rashid 168

Khouri, Raja 167, 168

Klein, Naomi 19, 23, 31–36, 121

Klein, Sherr Bonnie 121

Kristallnacht 59, 153

Lacelle, Nicole 14, 19, 33, 45–50, 53, 55, 59, 62–64, 71, 73, 74, 80–82, 84, 87–90, 92–95, 104, 134, 135, 138, 155, 158

Lacouture, Lucien 40–45

Leavitt, Melanie 1, 2, 4, 5, 7, 8, 18, 20, 59, 64, 76, 78, 80, 81, 85, 87, 90, 139, 140, 144

Leeder, Elizabeth 77–79, 84, 86

Lerman, Antony 168

lesbian activism 147, 148

Des lumières dans la Grande Noirceur (*A Vision in the Great Darkness*) (film) 15–17, 23, 24, 27, 28, 38, 41, 68, 82, 84, 96, 135, 153

Little Sister's Book and Art Emporium 123

Lorde, Audre 10, 11, 13, 148

Malatino, Hil 13

Mandela, Nelson 126–129

Mills, Rosewell 43, 44

Modern Book Shop, The 65–69, 74

Montreal (Quebec) 2–6, 9, 11, 14–16, 18–20, 30, 48, 62, 64, 78, 86, 147

Moraga, Cherríe 13, 148

Nasu, Masamoto 109–111

Nishimura, Shiego 109–111

None is Too Many (book) 152

optimism 138, 142

Owis, Bishop 13

Padlock Law 65, 67, 68, 85, 90

Paul, Eddie 33

Piepzna-Samarasinha, Leah Lakshimi 13

Pesotta, Rose 77–80, 82–86, 89, 94, 135

pornography 106, 120–123, 125

queer activism 13, 20, 125, 147, 148, 151

Racism 11, 31, 87, 88, 96, 125, 133, 145, 154

radiation 105, 106, 108–112

Radio Corporation of America (RCA) 90

Rebick, Judy 171

Ricci, Amanda 171

Roback, Fanny 24, 30

Roback, Harry 59

Roback, Isaac 23, 24, 25

Roback, Léa 1, 15, 19, 23, 30, 42, 47, 53, 67, 75, 83, 86, 91, 99, 131, 135, 138–141, 143, 150, 152, 157

Roback, Libby 23, 24, 25

Roback, Moishe 24, 25, 28

Robeson, Paul 140, 141, 145

Root, Maria 12

Rose, Fred 9, 25, 63–65, 74

Roskies-Goldstein, Louise 135, 137, 139

Roy, Gabrielle 91, 154

Schwartz, Susan 26, 99, 116, 117, 137

Setterington, Ken 58, 60

socialism 32, 151

social democrats 32, 54

Steinhouse, Berel 25, 38, 39, 48

Steinhouse, Sarah 25, 38, 39

Suffs 149

Taub, Shaina 149

The Love Booth and Six Companion Plays (playscript and audio-play) 147, 148, 151

trans activism 13, 125, 147, 151

Troper, Harold 152

Unwanted pregnancies 14, 112, 113, 114, 115, 116, 133

Uprichard, Lucy 43, 44

Verbatim theatre 147

Weisbord, Merrily 19, 55, 56, 67, 68, 69, 71, 141

Weissman, Aerlyn 124

Westley, Margaret 5, 6

Wilkinson, Jeffrey 167, 168

Winnipeg General Strike 61

Woodsworth, Judith 3, 24, 64, 70, 153

zionism 32–34

www.ingramcontent.com/pod-product-compliance
Lightning Source LLC
Chambersburg PA
CBHW070807230426
43665CB00017B/2515